ARE WE ALL HERE?

By the same author

Shakespeare's Journey Home: a Traveller's Guide Through Elizabethan England

Keeping Quiet: Visual Comedy in the Age of Sound

Coming Spring 2021: Water Gypsies: a History of Life on Britain's Waterways, The History Press.

Reviews of Julian Dutton's Keeping Quiet:

'A custard pie in the face of those who say slapstick is dead, by the go-to writer of British visual comedy,' – Harry Hill

"...a lovingly compiled and thorough history of the genre beyond the advent of sound,' – Jay Richardson. Chortle

JULIAN DUTTON

ARE WE ALL HERE?

a journey through the world's most curious clubs
& outlandish organisations

Treasurehouse Books

LONDON

Copyright © Julian Dutton

First Published 2020 by Treasurehouse Books.

The moral right of the author has been asserted.

All rights are reserved. No part of this publication may be reproduced, stored in a retrieval system or transmitted in any form or by any means, electronic, mechanical, photocopying, recording or otherwise, without the prior permission of the author, not be otherwise circulated in any form of binding or cover other than that in which it is published and without a similar condition including this condition being imposed upon the subsequent purchaser.

Set in Baskerville Old Face.

CONTENTS

Foreword

The Middlesex Advanced Rocketry Society
The Society of Dutch Balloon Twisters
The Wife-Carrying Society of Finland
The London Snuff Club
The English Subbuteo Table Football Association
The Glove
The Society for the Prevention of Cruelty to Insects
Friends of the Horse
National Vegetable Society
Society for the Public Understanding of the Middle Ages
The Elongated Collectors
The Regents Park Labour Party
The Free George Davis Society
The United Kingdom Lubricants Association
The Society of Hotel Bed Jumpers
The Made Up Textiles Association
The Esperance Club
Socialist Party of England & Wales (SPEW)
The Fairy Investigation Society
The Semi-Colon Appreciation Society
The Arctic Morris Dancing Group of Helsinki
The Telegraph Pole Appreciation Society
The Eccentric Club
The Beetle Fight Club
The Esperanto Society
The 'I Will Quit Society' of Blandford Forum

The American Headache Society
The Aetherius Society
The British Christmas Tree Grower's Association
English Society for Psychical Research
The Pylon Appreciation Society
The Exotic Animal Society
The Institute of Nanotechnology
The Ancient Order of Druids
The Prince Philip Movement
The Nuwaubian Society
Society for All Artists
Companions of the Crow
The Small Coal-man's Club
The Society for Creative Anachronism
The Split-Farthing Club
The Ejection Tie Club
The Association of Dead People
The League of Moveable Type
The Milton Keynes Ghost Club
The Man-Hunter's Club
The Beggar's Club
The Society for the Diffusion of Useful Knowledge
MI 14 – The Pigeon Secret Service
The Bilderberg Group

ACKNOWLEDGEMENTS

I am grateful to the Independent on Sunday Talk of the Town magazine where some of these articles originally appeared.

DEDICATION

To the first Neanderthal who opened his cave to a gathering of like-minded axe-collectors, rapped his flint gavel on a rock and declared 'meeting open.'

FOREWORD

It has been said of the English that they have always been "eminently clubbable." Whether that phrase originated from one or more of the many enemies we seem to have garnered over the centuries, chiefly the French, or whether it refers to our propensity for meeting in various huts up and down the country to discuss photography or hamsters, I do not know. I am plumping for the latter. It is understandable, therefore, for the majority of the entries in this volume to hail from our mad little island. But I have just six words to counter the notion that Britain has a monopoly of odd organisations - the Arctic Morris Dancing Society of Helsinki. Enough said. Many of the clubs in this book *are* British, but as our Finnish terpsichorean cousins demonstrate, eccentricity is not exclusive to our shores. It would be churlish, if not downright rude, if this volume were not to contain a small sprinkling of international ludicrousness. Over the past year I have travelled far and wide - mostly wide - in search of what I consider the oddest associations known to man, and this little book is the result of my journeying.

In its pages are contained edifying musings on some of the weirdest and most eccentric clubs ever to have parked their humdrum personas outside an obscure hall on a Friday evening, booted up their obsessions, waited for the excited hush to subside and declared *'meeting open.'*

First things first – what exactly is a club? And more importantly, *why* exactly is a club?

From time immemorial we have sought to bind ourselves to one another not simply through friendship or agreement – no, that has not been enough for us. We have always had the urge to go one step further and *form a society*. At bottom, the chief purpose of this society has probably been simply to give us something to do - but a consequence, foreseen or otherwise, has more often than not been to persuade others who have not yet been swayed to our cause to hop on at once and join us or face our wrath and scorn. Our club is serious. Its ambitions are worthy. I will only trust and speak to my fellow members; they understand me, you do not. Whether it's the British Humanist Society or the Chipping Norton Camera Club each member receives the same benefit from either – a wonderful sense of belonging; a little supra family in this harsh world of uncertainty and chaos. When I walk into the clubhouse, I feel wanted. I do not have to explain myself – we all know why we are there. It's in our constitution. Look – we have a pamphlet. This pamphlet will explain my life for a while.

The ultimate club, I suppose, is the church. Now that certainly *was* a club that was eager to persuade others to join. Not only did the early churchmen use the gentle arts of persuasion to attempt to make the unconverted hop aboard – if you refused, they burned you. Or threatened you with the fires of hell. Something of a hard sell, you might say. Nowadays, of course, they content themselves with the odd pamphlet. But even within the mighty church there are dozens and dozens of "sub-churches," clubs within clubs. I surmise that once the church got so big the feeling of belonging became somewhat diluted, so people like Wesley, Luther and the rest of them thought "hang on, I don't feel powerful and wanted enough in this club any more. I know – I'll hoof off and set my own one up. That'll show them."

Nowadays, of course, there are practically as many different churches are there are bridge clubs. Take London – its churches have a nasty habit of springing out on you in a startling fashion. Often they are hidden away, either squeezed anachronistically between shopping centres and bingo halls or set back from the main thoroughfare down a dark alleyway or cobbled courtyard. Sometimes they have strange names like *"The Holy Episcopalian Temple of the Divine King - non-Jesuitical branch,"* or *"The Sacred and Majestic Tabernacle of Zion."* Some are little more than tiny shacks of painted corrugated iron, with brightly coloured posters outside bearing the benevolent message - *"Repent ye your sins or ye shall burn in the everlasting damnation of hellfire and brimstone! Coffee Mornings twice weekly."* (Indeed, it appears to be one of the unwritten laws of church architecture that the humbler the edifice, the grander and more aspirational the name of the temple. I came across a small church in Tottenham called "The Most Holy Mercy-Seat of the Divine Ancient Covenant." It bore a striking resemblance to a scout-hut ripe for demolition.) And all of these fragmented "clubs," of course, are deadly rivals. I'm sure a *"Seventh Day Adventist"* wouldn't be caught dead conversing with an *"Eternal Friend of the Martyred Saviour."* And as for a member of the "Northern Baptist League" exchanging pleasantries with a "Blessed Little Sister of the Poor," well, I'm positive he'd sooner cross to the other side of the street, his umbrella lowered over his face.

In the early 1980's I flirted for a while with the "Worker's Revolutionary Party;" – well, I had fallen in with a rough lot at the British Museum where I was working. After attending a few dismal meetings it became increasingly clear that the people they hated more than anything else was not the ruling Capitalism, nor indeed the Conservative Government, but rather the Communist Party of Great Britain. At various demonstrations if one of these pariahs were spotted he would be hissed and booed like Captain Hook at a pantomime. At one memorable rally in Sloane Square I recall an unfortunate communist being chased down the Kings Road for having the audacity to sell a "C.P.G.B" badge. In the face of an indignant mob of WRP-ers, he threw his tray of badges in the air and legged it.

And that is the essence of the club. It is a descendant, of course, of the ancient tribe. Each tribe would have only been about twenty or forty strong, and my word we were a band of brothers! We miss all that. Our nations have got too big. Our countries no longer give us a great sense of belonging because more often than not there is too much to dislike about them.

So we join clubs. Of course, the *hobby club* is something of a different animal - people are united not over a cause, but an activity, be it Dog-grooming or the stories of Conan Doyle. I'm not sure the same level of bitter inter-club rivalry exists between these kinds of associations. That said, I'm sure if a member of the Ludlow Flower-Arranging Society were spotted exchanging clippings with the chair-lady of the East Shropshire Villages in Bloom Council, the incident would almost certainly be mentioned in severe tones at the next meeting.

This little book contains details of some of the strangest, funniest, most interesting, and quite frankly weirdest organisations ever to have convened in a scout-hut and elected one of themselves Chairperson. And if any of these collectives are met by the reader with a sceptical eyebrow, let me state at the outset with the phrase 'scout's honour' hovering on my lips: *every single club written about in this humble volume is true.*

Regretfully, of course, with such a plethora of battiness available, I had to leave many out. Many of the organisations that didn't make it in to the book had names like *"The Hoxton League For the Promotion of Mustard,"* and *"Wives Against Corsets."* Others that fell by the wayside were slightly less specific about their aims, like *"The High Wycombe Group."* What murky and mysterious ambitions did that association nurture? History does not say. Perhaps they were an early form of the now notorious "Bilderberg Group," before they got big and could meet in more prestigious surroundings like Brussels or Berne.

In the end I settled on fifty. Many of you will know of clubs that you feel sure should have made it on to the list, but a chart rundown such as this is inevitably a personal one.

I do not touch on the large and famous English Gentlemen's clubs – they are far too weighty for the sprightly, light-hearted aims of this volume. That said, one or two London clubs have wormed their way in, though by and large I have sought out only the weird and wonderful, the bizarre and the eccentric – for in desperation often lies delight. Who would not have paid handsomely to be at the inaugural meeting of the *"Ramsgate Satanic Society?"* or the *"Walsall Council for the Protection of Snakes?"*

I have also avoided some of those tiresome

University Clubs from both sides of the Atlantic like the Bullingdon or Princeton's 21 Club. Not only are they too well-known but to me they are insufferably dull, representing as they do – despite any largely fabricated mystique that surrounds them – simply the desire of a few privileged young men to get drunk and make other less fortunate folk clear up after them.

The following pages are a chronicle, if you will, of the deeply eccentric nature of the English and their international cousins – a pageant of the inadequate, the fanatical, the obsessed, the evangelical... and, well, the collector of cheese-labels.

For those you who like this book there are details in the endpapers of a society you can join. At the moment I call it "The Friends of Julian Dutton." Its membership will hopefully increase as a result of this little volume, though I am unconfident of competing successfully with Facebook. Its aims are simple, its intentions pure. Its first act will be to declare, in its constitution, a lifelong rivalry with the "Friends of Colin Woodall." Colin Woodall was a bully at my school. He needs teaching a lesson.

And only a club can do it.

The Middlesex Advanced Rocketry Society

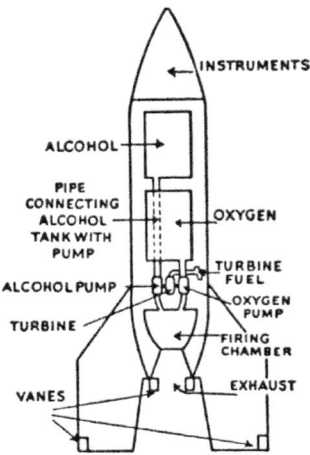

The Ruislip Wonderbus, designed by Harry Attercliffe, aged 51.

Now that NASA has shelved its Shuttle Space Programme this could well become the golden age for the Middlesex Advanced Rocketry Society, Pinner. Or - to give it its piquant acronym -

MARS. True, it might very well come up against some stiff competition from Soyuz, but surely that can serve only to make them stronger?

It is a little known fact that the hopes of the British contribution to the space race rests on the efforts of a small group of people beavering away in a quiet suburb fifteen miles west of London. The streets of Pinner are leafy, its houses generous. Its shops are friendly, its public amenities modest yet sufficient. Nothing about it cries out: "The conquest of the universe begins here!"

Yet despite the ordinariness of its location, please don't think the Middlesex Advanced Rocketry Society is just two men in a shed messing around with metal versions of those things your cat is afraid of on Firework Night. No, it's several men in a shed messing around with metal versions of those things your cat is afraid of on Firework Night. At least. Their membership could very well be in double figures. I don't know. They won't let me interview them.

I've been to Pinner. I've tried to find the Middlesex Advanced Rocketry Society. I've been unable to. Maybe they are like Area 51 – they exist, but when you try to penetrate them, they become elusive. When I walked around Pinner I was not stopped by any military types in jeeps brandishing guns. I was stopped by a woman who wanted to find out where the chemist's was. She didn't look like an astronaut. Indeed, nobody in Pinner looks like an astronaut. I imagine that when you visit NASA, you see at least one person whose gait and manner lends you to surmise an interstellar profession. And you find at least one person who salutes you.

Not in Pinner. No one in Pinner saluted me. They were indifferent to my presence.

The ambitions of the Middlesex Advanced Rocketry Society are murky to say the least. The moon? Mars? Cheshunt? The latter would perhaps seem more realistic given the levels of their technology; for as far as I can ascertain the propulsive abilities of the Society's finest rockets have yet to take them beyond the county boundary.

The addition of the word "Advanced" to their title is telling. Was there ever a "Middlesex *Intermediate* Rocketry Society?" Were their ambitions limited to entertaining the population on the anniversary of Guy Fawkes' demise? Or perhaps the Advanced lot are a splinter group. Fed up with the paltry aims of the intermediates, their minds fired by the International Space Station and the Hubble Telescope, a clean break was initiated at dead of night. Rocket parts, plans and tanks of fuel were summarily whisked from a shed at one end of Pinner to a shed on the other side of Pinner. A bigger one. More impressive. With a less leaky roof and a much better launching pad. So there.

And so the Advanced Rocketry Society carry out their cosmic work – seldom covered even by local news. Indeed, the media scarcely cover the international space efforts these days, so what chance has the Middlesex Rocketry Society got of gaining a slot on News at Ten, Advanced or otherwise?

So if you are motoring through western Middlesex one evening, try turning off the A40 as you approach Ruislip and take a detour through the leafy 1950's suburbia. It'll do you good. As you snake your way through the lamp lit streets, cast your eyes skyward. If you glimpse a golden streak, or a flash, or hear a bang and a low steady roar, do not fear. It is not Zeus giving vent to his meteorological ire. More than likely it is but the Middlesex Advanced Rocketry Society launching their latest bid to conquer the heavens. The heavens I tell you! The heavens!

The Society of Dutch Balloon Twisters

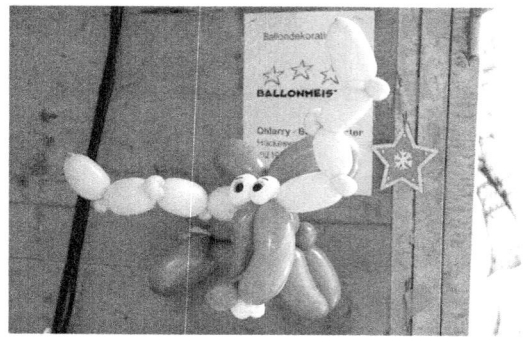

A poignant work by Hans Stoefflerssen entitled: 'Regrets.'

If you twist balloons and are Dutch then the chances are you are a member of the Society of Dutch Balloon Twisters. If not, then you are almost certainly some kind of rebel, a maverick in the balloon-twisting world, and the SDBT is probably much better off without you and your anti-social radicalism. Go and make your balloon animals in Cuba, we don't want you here.

I faintly remember balloon-twisting. When I was growing up it seemed to form part of the school curriculum. Every now and then, in between lessons, there would be some kind of occasion in the hall, and a feature of it would be a middle-aged man in an ill-fitting suit making sausage dogs out of inflatable plastic. Sometimes he made giraffes. But mostly sausage dogs. Camels must have been trickier – I never saw a camel.

I don't see many balloon-twisters around much these days. Are they a dying craft, like knife-grinders and chimneysweeps? Did they go the way of the miners? Are they the forgotten victims of the economic revolution of the 1980's? Did Margaret Thatcher order police baton charges on hundreds of striking balloon-twisters? Were they hauled into the backs of police vans screaming 'Get your hands off my sausage dog?'

They had a union here in the UK: The National Association of Balloon Artists (NABA). But perhaps they were led by a balloon-twisting version of Arthur Scargill, and the Conservative Government wanted nothing better than to see him destroyed along with all the other 'beer and sandwiches' brigade. For NABA, I am reliably informed, is no more. Its former leader, Oscar the Clown, ekes out his last bitter days in an old folk's home in Bolton, showing his giraffe to anyone who cares to see it.

But in the Netherlands balloon-twisters obviously had a brighter future. They didn't go on strike without a secret ballot. They weren't secretly funded by an obnoxious Libyan dictator. They just quietly and peacefully plied their art in schools and halls up and down – or rather across, if we're talking of the Netherlands – their grateful nation. Like clog-making and the manufacture of marijuana cigarettes, balloon manipulation has survived as a craft in Holland into the twenty-first century. To be a balloon twister and to be Dutch, therefore, is to be happy.

Are there any animals peculiar to Holland that the Dutch balloon-twister can make that his British counterpart cannot? Certain snakes, no doubt, given the paucity of those creatures in these islands. The Rotterdam Filligrew Snake? The Groningen Hedgehog? I've just made those up. I just don't know. There, I've said it.

One characteristic of balloon artists, of course, is that they all have extremely powerful lungs. An inevitable consequence of their chosen art. They develop, over the years, massive upper bodies. Some of them turn into freaks and have to be hidden away in secret hospitals. This is where the Dutch Balloon Twisting Society comes in – I am told that they fund various clandestine medical centres up and down Holland where victims of 'Giant Lung Syndrome,' as it is called, can go for a lung-reducing operation. Balloon twisters book into the clinic looking like Charles Atlas and come out resembling Twiggy. It's remarkable. I've met some of them. Of course once they've had the operation they can never go back to balloon-twisting. Their new small lungs are just not up to it. They can scarcely come up with a prawn, let alone a sausage dog.

So if you are a young person on the threshold of life and are about to go in for your first Career Guidance interview at school – and if, when seated before your mentor, a sudden vision floats before you in the form of a cylindrical inflated orange dachshund – then balloon twisting must be for you. It's a calling, a vocation, like nursing or bookmaking. But let me give you one piece of advice. Pretend to be Dutch. To be Dutch and a Balloon-twister, is to be protected.

The Wife-Carrying Society of Finland

At the outset I must assert that they do not carry their wives all the time. That would smack of a certain deficiency in the character of the wife, not to say a marked streak of the primitive in the husband.

No - the carrying takes place on special occasions. During races, to be exact. I am reliably informed that organised spousal haulage takes place across the world, from Estonia to North America. I have chosen Finland, simply because they were the founders of this close contact sport.

What, Why, How? – I hear you cry. Calm down. No need to shout. Well, let's start with the what. Wife-Carrying originated in Finland in the early nineteenth century and is the practice of slinging ones loved one over the shoulders and running with her through an obstacle course. Over walls, through marshes, across rivers – you know what an obstacle is. You name a geographical feature, the Finns hauled their better halves through it.

Now for the 'why.' Well, tales have been passed down from one person to another about a man named Herkko Rosvo-Ronkainen. This man was considered a robber in the late 1800s, lived in a forest, and ran around with his gang of thieves causing harm to the villages. There are three ideas to why/how this sport was invented. First, Rosvo-Ronkainen and his thieves were accused of stealing food and women from villages in the area he lived in; then carried these women on their backs as they ran away, (hence the "wife" or women carrying). For the second idea, it has been said that young men would go to villages near their own, steal other men's wives, and then have the woman become their own wife. These wives were also carried on the backs of the young men; this was referred to as "the practice of wife stealing." Lastly, there was the idea that Rosvo-Ronkainen trained his thieves to be "faster and stronger" by carrying big, heavy sacks on their backs, which could have eventually evolved to a sport because of the hard labour (endurance), and muscle strengthening; which most sports ensure.

Whichever is the truth – and it's probably an amalgamation of all three – this Rosvo-Ronkainen chappie sounds a thoroughly unpleasant fellow all round, and not the sort you'd invite round for a dinner party. You'd be afraid to turn your back. One pop into the kitchen to replenish the plate of nibbles and he'd sling your missus over his shoulder and be off. You'd be afraid to lower your eyes to the Trivial Pursuit game for fear he'd haul her off through the French Windows.

We move on to the 'How.'

There are, of course, different schools of thought within the world of Wife-Carrying, chiefly involving the method of elevation. The classic Finnish style involves the accommodating wife clamping her spouse's neck in a kind of scissors movement, and hanging down his back. The second is the universally known Fireman's lift, where the willing female is thrown over the shoulder; and the third is the good old Piggy-Back. This latter sounds the most comfortable for the woman, but is not the most popular largely because it makes you look like you're in a parent's race at a school sports day.

Rolf Ninverssen has been carrying his wife for more than ten years. I don't mean up the stairs or round the shops. He puts her down occasionally. At his practice session in his back garden on the outskirts of Helsinki his better half hangs from him like some kind of human necklace, while he demonstrates his sport.

As he gallops up and down his garden I cannot help but admire Mrs. Ninverssen. And not because she is lying upside down presenting her rear end in a most seductive way to anyone who cares to look. No, it strikes me as a I watch her bouncing up and down and to and fro, that to submit to half an hour or more of this husband-haulage it is clear that one must have *absolute trust* in ones carrier.

I put this to her over tea and Madeleine cakes after the demonstration is over.

Mrs. Ninverssen - her breath fully recovered - nods and smiles. She then jokes that it is best never to row with ones' man the night before a contest.

Have there been cases of wives being deliberately dropped in swamps, mid-race, as a result of a pre-match tiff?

"It has happened many times," replies Rolf, a glint in his eye.

As I say goodbye to Mr. & Mrs. Ninversson I muse that perhaps wife-carrying is the recipe for a sound marriage. If you know for certainty that your husband is, once a month, going to carry you across a river, then the chances are you not going to swear and rail at him the night before. And if you are an ambitious sportsman whose aim for most of your adult life has been to win your local wife-carrying championship, then the last thing you want to do is for her to - yards away from the finishing line – loosen her grip, slide down your body into the river and swim off, laughing, all because over dinner three days ago you criticised her taste in cushion covers.

I shall contact Relate at once and recommend they include the promotion of Wife-Carrying in their counselling sessions for estranged couples.

I may very well take up the sport myself. First, though, I'd better find myself a wife. It wouldn't do to grab any woman and carry her off. It's not done any more. Questions would be asked.

No one had the heart to tell Olaf he'd dropped his wife half a mile back.

The London Snuff Club

"Give me wine, women and snuff, until I cry out – hold, enough!" Not, perhaps, as profound or as well known as his ruminations upon the nightingale, but nevertheless penned by Keats himself. For Adonis too, along with such diverse figures as Queen Victoria and Grimaldi the Clown, was a lover of that nasal stimulation we have come to know as snuff.

'Snuff ? You mean that strange brown powdery mixture we used to see our Grandfathers taking as they sat in their big floral armchairs, in a strange ritual involving the extraction of a small shiny box from their waistcoats, a soft *click!*, a pinching of stubby thumb and forefinger, a loud snort, followed seconds later by an elephantine sneeze ? Nobody takes snuff today, surely!'

Wrong. For according to the proprietors of G. Smith & Sons Snuff Shop, formerly of Charing Cross Road - London's oldest purveyor of powdered nasal excitement and the occasional venue for the meetings of the shadowy London Snuff Club - the habit of inserting this (perfectly legal) substance into one's nostril cavities is not only still indulged in but is growing rapidly in popularity, in particular with the under-forties. To understand why, I paid a visit to this cramped, Victorian establishment squeezed crookedly between dusty bookshops on the Charing Cross Road, before it sadly closed. Obviously before it closed.

The shop door swung shut behind me with a muffled *tinkle* of brass bell. The noise of the West End receded. And with it vanished the twenty-first century.

I found myself in a dark, sallow, tobacco-coloured shop facing a dark, sallow, tobacco-coloured shop assistant - straight out of Dickens. He smiled and bowed slightly like Uriah Heep,

All around me were exhaled the gentle, slightly sweet perfumes of snuff jars and tightly packed *Abdullah* cigarettes imported from Turkey. On the walls were what at first glance looked like faded Victorian circus posters, but which on closer inspection were making the proud boast that G. Smith was a leading "Importer of Havana, Mexican, Indian and Manila Cigars."

"Tobacco Year Books" from 1940 sat alongside, incongruously, the works of Longfellow. Huge pot-bellied bell-jars stood stacked on the
endless shelves, each packed with a powder of different colour and texture - rusty brown, ochre, fawn, earth-dark, pale wood-thatch. And the names, like a litany of spells from some old tome - *Macouba, Old Paris, Santo Domingo...* brands of a bygone age - *Cafe Royale, Princes Dark,*

Wild Strawberry - each boasting its own scent - *Saville,* a dry light snuff flavoured with orange; *Attar of Roses* for the lover of sweetness.

"We sell pounds of the stuff," boasted Uriah Heep, whose real name was Jeff; "and I mean pounds in weight. Sometimes I look at all these big jars and think to myself – every bit of it's going to end up in someone's conk. Hard to believe really. Was that two ounces sir?"

He scooped a small silver trowel into one of the jars and deposited a few ounces of *Spanish S.B.* (I don't know what the S.B. stands for, but you can bet it's stronger than your plain *Spanish*) into a twist of paper. A businessman in navy blue pinstripe popped the small pyramid in his breast pocket and sidled furtively out of the shop.

Golden Cardinal, Dr. James Robertson Justice, Mortlaix... Despite its romantic soubriquets, snuff, however, still suffers from an image problem.

"I suppose it's still a bit odd. It was never as glamorous as smoking – at least, the way the old movies made smoking glamorous. Though it's less anti-social and, some say, less harmful."

Indeed. There have been articles defending snuff in the 'Lancet,' no less.

Yet you rarely see anyone taking it. But according to G. S. Smith & Sons this is a boom time for snuff. From the eager tone of the retailer I chatted with one fully expects it soon to be traded on the stock market along with oil and pork bellies. Snuff millionaires will have houses built in Essex in the shape of huge noses. The ban on smoking in public places has resulted in a boom.

So where are all these new snuff-takers ? Obviously doing their snuffing in private. Or in the back-room of the shop, where the meetings of the London Snuff Club take place. I am not permitted to pass through the door to the club-room. Perhaps it is a door that opens into a secret magical Edwardian kingdom.

And there's the rub. There's still seems to be something vaguely exciting, vaguely *illicit* about snuff-taking. It smacks of opium dens and Edwardian detectives, secret societies and shadowy villains. Even some of the slogans on the posters: *"Bordeaux – piquant and refreshing, it never cloys and is a favourite with the heavy user"* - suggest an affinity with substances plainly more illegal.

So maybe that's the reason for snuff's growing popularity. In an age when you can stroll down the Brixton High Road puffing brazenly on a joint, confident that the worst you will receive is a 'tut-tut' from a benign constable and the gentle wagging of an admonitory finger, then perhaps the ritual of snuff-taking offers a more esoteric high.

It's time to try some. My nasal tutor is gentle with me, proffering a simple pinch of *Café Royale*, reputedly the most expensive snuff in the world. Manufactured from a special blend of North American and Oriental tobaccos, it is perfumed with pure coffee essence. The effect, I have to say, is rather akin to shoving a teaspoonful of Maxwell House up your hooter. For a few minutes my eyes are watery, my brain ablaze. It is like having a small firework going off inside your head. Uriah brings me down from my coffee high with a small twist of *Wild Strawberry*, a light medium milled snuff designed for the novice. It is a bit like having dessert after the coffee. I ask him if there is any beef flavoured snuff, enabling one to make a four-course meal of the thing. He doesn't reply.

I snort my way across Europe and the Americas, from *Old Paris* to *Santo Domingo*. While the wine-taster spits between sips, the snuffer blows. I make a mental note to destroy my handkerchief afterwards.

By the end of the session I am light-headed yet strangely vibrant. In the dim quiet of the shop, I feel like a *fin-de-siecle* rake who has tasted the sinful pleasures of a limehouse opium den.

Which is maybe the whole point about snuff. As Uriah Heep bids me goodbye and I re-enter the twenty-first century din outside, I muse that in ten years time when we've tired of being able to purchase a neatly-rolled joint at Starbucks along with our *espresso macchiato*, then perhaps we'll be lured into seeking the darker, more romantic domain of the *Snuff-Café*. Londoners will sit hunched over their chrome tables, alternately sipping frothy cappuccinos and entertaining their conks to a selection of snuffs just as varied as the coffees.

I pat my pocket. Secreted there is a small round box full of Smith's *Kendal Brown* and a membership application form for the London Snuff Club. Seduced by the salesmanship of G. Smith & Sons, I am determined to spearhead snuff's glorious revival. All I need now is the wine and the women.

Snuff is renowned for imparting a pleasing, attractive temperament to the user.

The English Subbuteo Table Football Association

The Subbuteo Cup Final, 2020, seconds before violence tore through the stadium.

I have just returned from my first Subbuteo Cup Final, and I will never be attending another. I am a shaken man. I was lucky to escape with my life. I have rarely attended a real football match in my life, let alone one consisting of miniature plastic figures. I imagined it would be a calm, carefree occasion, civilised, good-humoured and jovial.

Not a bit of it. If I say to you chairs were flung and noses bloodied, you'll have a slight inkling of the kind of afternoon I've had.

I am, of course, aware that the odd shindig takes place at actual football matches. But in the town hall in Winnersh, Berkshire, in the presence of at least three dignitaries from the local Rotary Club? It beggars belief.

I arrived at 2.30pm on a sunny afternoon and was given tea and a fairy cake. So far so good. All very civilised. The 'teams' arrived. By teams I mean, of course, two men. That was fine. It was their supporters that proved the problem. About two hundred of them turned up, in coach-loads – all wearing scarves and shouting out their team songs. As soon as I saw them I knew – I get these gut instincts – that a cup of tea and a fairy cake each would probably do very little to quench their high spirits. These weren't fairy cake kind of people. Some people aren't. I forgave them that. But what I did not forgive was them producing numerous cans of lager from dozens of carrier bags and proceeding to neck them with the seeming thirst of John Mills in 'Ice Cold in Alex.'

Nor did the organisers – the referee, linesmen and so on. Several of them were frowning. But frowning was not sufficient. The fans paid no attention to the frowns. So, the early drunkenness notwithstanding, the match began. Kick-off was without incident. I say 'kick-off' – I mean, of course, 'flick-off.' For those unfamiliar with Subbuteo, the game is played by what can only be described as a hefty (yet skilful) nudging with the forefinger of one of your men. This propels the ball – seemingly uncontrollably – across the felt pitch towards, hopefully, one of your other men, and ultimately, into the back of the tiny net.

Often the ball doesn't go towards one of your other men. Often it goes wherever it wants. That's the nature of random imparted motion. Blame Isaac Newton – I think he discovered it. The fans didn't blame Isaac Newton. They blamed their opponents' fans. Volleys of yells and screaming followed each random flick.

And when, seven minutes into the game, Winnersh scored, well – all hell broke loose. Chairs were thrown, fairy cakes stamped on. I had to take cover and shield my slice of Victoria sponge with my match programme.

And this was only the first goal. As the first half proceeded, so too did the ferocity of the supporters increase, almost exponentially one might say.

And it didn't stop at vocal violence and excessive demonstrations of loyalty. These 'fans' take the game of Subbuteo so seriously that they have fashioned small plastic models of rioters, which they proceeded to invade the pitch with, throwing them on the baize like manic chicken-feeders scattering corn to a mob of starving hens. The referee bravely countered this pitch invasion by producing a small plastic model of his own – a single police constable. This miniscule officer, this paltry peeler, sadly proved no match for the marauding dolls he was facing. In brief, this tiny symbol of authority was ejected from the stadium like a pea shot from a pea-shooter's gun, to land on the floor of the town hall some twenty feet away – the equivalent, if you scale it up, of an actual human policeman being thrown from Wembley to Perivale.

The scene was hideous. I, amongst the other civilised spectators such as the sports correspondent of the Winnersh Bugle and Mrs. Tillotson the caretaker's wife who made the tea and supplied the fairy cakes, retired to the corner of the hall, our faces resembling the protagonist in Edvard Munch's scream.

The last thing I remember is the pitch itself being pulled from the table like the *denouement* of some crazy magic trick, and the players being scattered across the parquet flooring. Mrs. Tillotson and I retired to the kitchens - where she consoled me with another fairy cake - and we were led out of a secret back entrance.

I learned later that the cause of the supporter's ire was a recent transfer of one of the challenging team's key players – one Rudy Stifgarten, a striker whose transfer was viewed nothing less than a defection. The transfer fee was a mere £8.50, but it clearly rankled. The mob were there to destroy the game, and destroy it they did.

As I said goodbye in the car-park to the Sports Correspondent of the Winnersh Bugle who, shaken though he was, was already scribbling his copy in a Staple's notebook, I made a mental note of my own never to attend a football match again, miniature or otherwise. The participants in the contest may have been tiny, but the passions were huge. Human beings have vast reservoirs of emotion bubbling deep within them like larva, and if all it takes is a small plastic doll to release that pent-up aggression into an eruption of Vesuvian proportions – and in Winnersh no less – then God help us all.

The Glove

Perhaps the most oddly named club in this variegated chronicle, the mysteriously-named 'Glove' was an offshoot of the Royal Geographical Society, an eccentric group of London financiers in the early twentieth century whose aim was to pool their resources and fund foreign expeditions, chiefly to South America. One of the most famous recipients of their largesse was the legendary explorer Colonel Percy Fawcett, whose last and apparently fatal trip was funded by the mysterious 'Glove' in 1925.

The motives of the Glove were clearly fired by dreams of finding El Dorado, the legendary lost city of gold – or rather Fawcett's equivalent, which he rather unimaginatively called the city of 'Z.'

A larger-than-life figure in the Kipling mould, Fawcett was a friend of Conan Doyle and Rider Haggard – indeed, his early expeditions had inspired the former's famous book 'The Lost World.' Every time Fawcett nipped over to the Brazilian jungle – which was as regularly as you and I hop on the train to work – he seemed to find something remarkable, chiefly in form of some bizarre new animal. Upon his return he would regale his fellow members of the Royal Geographical Society with tales of seeing the Double-Nosed Dog, an Anaconda 62 ft long; or the giant Apazauca spider.

Inspired by these colourful anecdotes – and some genuine discoveries of geographical importance such as the source of the Heath River on the border of Peru and Bolivia – the Glove were even more enthused when Fawcett expressed his belief in the existence of the mysterious Lost City of 'Z.' In 1925 they financed his biggest – and what proved to be his final – trip to the dark heart of the Brazilian jungle.

What happened on that last fateful journey has passed into expeditionary folklore, and has been the subject of countless books, TV documentaries and, indeed, further explorations. Suffice to say, Fawcett did not return, and legion have been the theories behind his disappearance. No less than one hundred explorers have died in an attempt to find Fawcett, despite him having left explicit instructions not to send anyone should he not return. He sent a final telegraph to his wife on September 29th 1925 saying he was about to set off up the Upper Xingu, an offshoot of the Amazon, into hitherto unknown territory; together with his son Jack and his fellow explorer Raleigh Rimmel.

None of the men were ever seen again. Rumours abounded: he was living deep in the jungle being worshipped as some kind of white god; he had been killed by natives because he had lost his boat-load of gifts – a dire breakage of protocol which must have incensed the natives, who adored their compasses, mirrors and other trinkets. In more recent times, TV crews from all over the world have journeyed upriver and questioned members of the remote tribes still living there, to try and trace any memory of the fate of this extraordinary Englishman. And an oral tradition does exist within these communities, of a trio of 'mysterious white men' who visited the Kalapolos tribe in the 1920's, and who then penetrated even deeper into the jungle in search of a monumental city that they, the Kalapolos themselves, had heard of but never seen. The white men vanished - killed, so the Kalapolos say, by the 'Fierce Men of the Jungle.'

Bones have been found, and discounted. Items belonging to Fawcett's party – a chronometer, a knife – have been discovered over the years in the possession of various tribesmen; but they could have been given as gifts on any one of Fawcett's numerous previous expeditions. His disappearance even inspired the brother of Ian Fleming, Peter, to mount his won expedition which resulted in the best-selling and extremely aptly titled "In Search of Colonel Fawcett." So many expeditions mounted to look for him have been fatal that it's surprising there isn't a book entitled "In Search of the Searchers for Colonel Fawcett."

And the 'Glove?' Well, they too have faded into obscurity, their money presumably dissipated into other crazy schemes like the search for the Holy Grail or the Great White Whale. Perhaps their descendants still meet in various clubhouses or snug bars in the City of London, and toast the last of their protégées – and indeed perhaps the last Gentleman Adventurer of the twentieth century - Colonel Percy Fawcett.

The redoubtable Fawcett in one of his happier moments: his wedding, 1921

The Society for the Prevention of Cruelty to Insects

Ralph Appleby, Honorary President of the Society for the Prevention of Cruelty to Insects, writing a stiff letter to Baxter's Fly-Swatters Ltd.

I love insects. I have to say that - there are more of them than me. They could gang up. Some of them aren't particularly attractive, it's true - but then again we probably don't appear very alluring to a gnat. That said, there is one trying to woo me at this very moment. Her methods are persistent but will be ultimately fruitless. I'm not marrying her, and that's that. She'll have to be told.

I also have to confess, without duress I may add, that I have always been possessed of a fervent desire not to hurt them. Sometimes – especially at school – this has led me into some awkward situations. I recall one particular incident in the science block of Great Marlow School, Buckinghamshire. Tommy Wood hit a fly and I, who would never hit a fly, instead hit Tommy Wood. Tommy Wood didn't understand this, so he gave me a bloody nose.

So my credentials are impeccable as regards being a worthy guardian of the rights of the six-legged. However, my sense of protective duty towards our winged companions as we journey together – sometimes too closely – through this vale of tears has never extended to the desire to join and actively participate in a society devoted to ensuring their safety. That might well be a deficiency on my part. You tell me.

Have insects themselves ever demanded such a society? No. They've never felt the need. Why is this? Well, it's blindingly clear they are a protective society in themselves. They have stings, bites, very clever escape capabilities, and what is perhaps their most powerful weapon - sheer numbers. There are so many of the blighters that should they lose one or two they simply smirk, and show us another of their kind. "You think we care?" they say, preening themselves, "that you just trod on Ronald the ant? There's plenty more where he came from mate. May I present – Ronald's eight million children!"

The Society's website itself hints at this problem in a sideways manner by declaring "precious little is being done to protect them." Pardon me for living. Why, I wonder, do you think that is? Could it be that they don't *need* protecting? Let's face it, even if every single human being on earth were an unspeakable sadist and spent their entire day going round stamping and swatting and crushing, I doubt that the population of insects on earth would be even be dented. Whole weekend events of insect-baiting could be arranged – towns and cities could have "Anti-Insect Days," – and yet their numbers would not be depleted. They would be like those Zulus in the film – what was it called? – oh yes, "Zulu." Just when Stanley Baker and Michael Caine think they've vanquished most of them, up pop another ten thousand from over the horizon. That's insects. They're laughing at us. Let's just be thankful they don't have spears.

Do the insects feel demeaned and patronised that there is a Society devoted to their protection? Attempted interviews have not yielded results. I'm guessing they are largely indifferent. But it is probably not them who benefits anyway – the existence of the Society is there, and rightfully so, for the spiritual and moral enrichment of us marauding, cruel, insect-crushing humans. And long may it be so.

Friends of the Horse

At first glance this noble society might appear to be an association dedicated in some way to a form of equine pampering. Taking a couple of distressed ponies on holiday perhaps, or providing therapy to a colt suffering from self-doubt. But in truth the founding members of "Friends of the Horse" had a deeper, more serious purpose.

By the early 1900's the motor-car was proving a threat to the four-legged transport system of old England. True, there were only a few hundred vehicles on the road, but horses began understandably to get a trifle nervous. Some more prescient amongst them started to root around for alternative employment. Their opportunities were limited. Politics was certainly out. A couple of enterprising mares opened a teashop in Dorset. It failed. What could horses do apart from pull human beings along in carts and carriages, or drag a plough across a muddy field? The answer came back to them, and was deafening: nothing. Older horses, loitering idly on street-corners, began reminiscing sadly to frisky fillies at their side.

"Back in the day," they would whinny, "this highway would have rattled with the noise of a dozen grand coaches, drawn by a throng of shining steeds. Your Uncle Lionel was one of them. Where is he now? In the form of glue he now holds together the spines of fifty books. It's not the same...."

And so the Friends of the Horse was born. True, it was a human being who began it, but doubtless the horses approved. What else could they do? – they were on a hiding to nothing. Did the horses express gratitude? History does not tell us. My feeling is that they were probably indifferent. After all, did they reciprocate when men had their jobs threatened by mechanisation? Did a group of stallions in Berkshire form "Friends of the Human," when several dozen farm-workers were laid off to be replaced with the combine harvester? For a few short years the "Friends of the Horse" threatened to become as powerful a force in British politics as Kier Hardie's nascent Labour Party. Demonstrations marched – or rather clip-clopped – on Downing Street. Petitions were handed in, both signed and hoof-printed. An ambitious mare even stood for election as MP for Corby South. But the Society was not to realise its place in the sun. In 1889 there were a mere 572 cars in the whole world, today, there are 600 million – that is to say, one car per eleven people. I have a Smart car, and getting those eleven people in is no easy thing. It is reasonable therefore to say that the "Friends of the Horse" were fighting a losing battle. With the repeal of the Red Flag Act in 1896 when cars were permitted to travel at more than 4 miles per hour, a cloud of doom settled over the indolent nag. By the end, the society's numbers were so low it had to be renamed "Friend of the Horse." Does it exist today? In a word, no.

'He's done this to patronise me, I can sense it.'

The National Vegetable Society

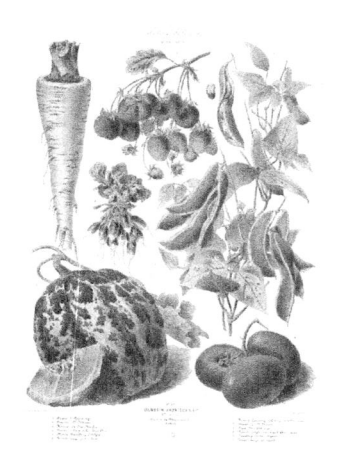

Several beautiful vegetables pose for a glamour shot.

There is a certain pagan frisson to our love of vegetables, though the spiritual significance of the root-crop is now obscured somewhat by our veneration of the vitamin. In the twenty-first century the humble cabbage is perceived as simply a fine source of iron and fibre, yet to our

Celtic forefathers it was nothing less than a god in crinkly leaf form. Ancient Priests burned incense to welcome in the harvest, supplicants knelt before onions, and women in various states of idolatrous ecstasy offered up prayers for the resurrection of the divine courgette.

Today, however, the National Vegetable Society is not headed by a Druid, but a panel of horticulturalists, or "Rootarians," as they are jocularly known amongst the members. They are a fine body of people, and do wonderful work. It is not a little puzzling, however, to learn that the National Vegetable Society is a charity.

Now I know everything can be a charity these days, from schools to areonautical engineering firms – bung "Registered Charity" on your notepaper and off slinks the taxman down your garden path cursing and gnashing his officious teeth. But vegetables? They have their own marketing boards, and good luck to them. I can understand the Marketing Board. But *charity?* Do carrots suffer religious persecution? Are radishes bullied by turnips? Is the potato inwardly tortured by the rise of the processed food? Is there is an orphanage for asparaguses in Redditch? I'm only asking.

Do vegetables suffer? Some of the more hardened vegans of course believe it is indeed so. Some, god bless them, weep silently as they pass allotments; burn with indignation at the sight of the word "salad," and swoon at the very thought of pureed swede. Quite frankly I don't know what's left for them to eat. Soil?

Each year the National Vegetable Society produces a volume of poetry. I have the latest edition in front of me. Godfrey Duplex's "Eulogy for a Chopped Carrot" is particularly moving. And I challenge you to read Madelaine Allbright's "Mashed Potato is Genocide" without shaking with sobs.

I learn that some members of the Society believe that vegetables can speak. I'm not going to name them. They know who they are. Now, I myself am not scientifically trained, but I can be pretty confident in asserting that marrows don't possess vocal cords. Although it was never explicitly stated in any of my school biology lessons, the fact that radishes couldn't sing nevertheless hovered in the background as a kind of accepted sub-text. We all assumed it was a given. Ah yes, these extreme members of the Vegetable Society will say – but our little green companions don't *need* vocal chords. They employ far more subtle techniques of communication. Scent, vibration, and such like.

I've never had a conversation with a caper. I've never discussed philosophy with a leek. Don't get me wrong – I'd like to. There's nothing I'd enjoy more than a hearty political debate across the breakfast table with a Savoy Cabbage. Call me narrow minded but I just can't envisage it happening. But if these hard-core vegetable-rights fellows are right, and they *can* converse, then of course they should be afforded a political voice. Their opinions must be heard. The vote? Well... I think the day I see a Cos Lettuce in the polling booth is the day when I begin to suffer a certain shakiness vis-à-vis my faith in democracy. But... one could adapt. Votes for men, women, animals, vegetables, bring them all on. I'll wager the ultimate aim of the National Vegetable Society is to see a Garden Pea in Number Ten Downing Street, and I for one will not begrudge someone a wild street party when that worthy dream is finally realised.

Society for the Public Understanding of the Middle Ages

Of all things I feel the public are in need of better understanding of, it's the Middle Ages. I've always felt this. Whenever I've come across the public – I try to avoid it but at times it is tricky, especially in shopping centres – whenever I bump into them I come away from the encounter weighed down with a sense of dispiritedness. The sole source of my mild depression is that their understanding of European history between the years 900AD to 1500 just doesn't cut the mustard.

I can take people's selfish parking habits, their swearing, even their chain-smoking – but their lack of knowledge about the dynastic problems that beset Edward I and his offspring in the years immediately following the signing of the Magna Carta – well, it fair makes my blood boil. Every time a member of the *hoi polloi* demonstrates a lack of grasp of the subtle political nuances of the life of Eleanor of Aquitaine, or the role of usury in the rise of the international cloth trade, I want to curse them. There've been several close calls in various pubs in the Greater London area –

arguments over the accuracy of the Bayeux tapestry, or the 'Richard of Gloucester, Saint or Sinner?' controversy – that have nearly resulted in blows, but such confrontations have, thankfully, ended in only a few smashed glasses and a reluctant handshake.

I do not hit them. I simply gnash my teeth and withdraw from the encounter. I'm not insane.

I've often thought of setting up a Society for the Public Understanding of the Middle Ages myself. But such thoughts have usually been quelled by a good game of golf. As a boy I flirted with the idea, but decided to join the school dramatic society instead. So imagine my delight when I discovered that some jolly decent coves had embraced the challenge, knuckled down and gone and set up the thing for me.

'My massacre of the Burgundians has been gravely misunderstood.'

I would join, but apparently they meet in Kalamazoo. Kalamazoo sounds as though it is some kind of mythical country, like Noel Langley's Land of Green Ginger, or Frank L. Baum's Oz. But I'm reliably informed it is in Michigan. I can't pop over to Michigan every time I want to make a point about the Middle Ages. That would smack of obsession.

So I wish them luck from afar. I shall be assessing the effectiveness of the society's work by periodically stopping a member of the public in the street and giving them a good grilling on 'Monastic literature of the Dark Ages,' or the Hundred Years' War. If they look at me askance and move off briskly, I shall be writing PUMA a stiff letter.

The Elongated Collectors

At the outset it must be pointed out that the members of this Society are not themselves elongated. Their meetings do not take place in halls with very high ceilings. No stooping takes place. Their arms are not possessed of the same stretching ability as that talented fellow from the Fantastic Four.

No, the fully paid up subscribers of the Elongated Society *collect* elongated things. Not *every* elongated thing – that would be eccentric. They do not seek any old stretchable object that exists in this odd world – like worms, rubber bands, or the time it takes to finish an assignment. They collect - and only collect - elongated *coins.*

Before you flip the page in disgust, imagining I have made all this up, be warned: the society for the collection of elongated coins is a serious organisation, and your scepticism could lead to severe repercussions. They are extremely earnest in their work. It is a very solemn and important business. It is a respected branch of numismatics, and has its very own name: exonumia.

Now to the uninitiated exonumia sounds remarkably like that form of chest infection I had earlier in the year. In fact, I am sure my Doctor uttered the word - or something very similar - in his surgery after my examination. Unless he was drawing attention to his collection of elongated coins. Though I doubt it. I didn't notice a long display case containing any form of money - stretched or otherwise - amongst the posters urging us to lower our cholesterol or to feed our babies with our breasts.

From what strange nation do these malleable tokens of exchange originate? What country uses elongate coins? A sort of loopy Salvador Dali-land, where not only the clocks are soft but also the currency? A Kingdom where flexibility is not only respected but revered? Where all the leaders are tall? Where gymnastics is the national sport and dachsunds the mascots at every fixture?

Before launching into an investigation of the Society itself, a certain question must surely be put: why stretch coins in the first place? I would never address such a question to a member of TES. I would probably be met with glazed eyes and an almost imperceptible sigh. Such a response would tell me immediately that this poor fellow has been asked this question many hundreds, if not thousands of times. And the answer has always been the same. A single word: commemoration.

To mark a great occasion or deed, an ordinary coin is apparently not enough. No, only an elongated coin will do. When in some dim and misty decade of Roman hegemony a coin-smith was instructed to make a medal commemorating the noble massacre by Severus Maximus of two hundred innocent Celts who'd been minding their own business just outside Portsmouth, he might have thought to himself – hang on. I saw that battle. It was great. An ordinary coin isn't enough – no, dammit, I'm going to stretch it.

And so the elongated coin was born. And as night follows day, where elongated coins are, a Society dedicated to their collection must follow.

Are some coins more elongated than others? Of course. How ridiculous of you to even think of asking that question. The more memorable the event, surely the longer the coin must be. The opening of Pickford Town Hall in 1821 was marked by the minting of a coin that one could scarcely apply the appellation 'stretched,' let alone 'elongated.' To the inexpert eye one would not even admit it into any display case, let alone the hallowed "Museum of Exonumia." Yet the Charge of the Light Brigade – well, that gave rise to a coin almost as long as the Charge itself. It was elongated to the point of transparency. Long halls had to be hired for its display. Eighteen men carried it inside. It was so elongated that people quite frankly got fed up with it. Few men saw both ends of the coin, such was its lack of brevity. The weather was often completely different at either end: storms at one end, sultry sunshine at the other.

And yet it was not the most elongated coin in history. No. There is a Holy Grail amongst members of TES. Its very existence is doubted by all except the very dreamiest of enthusiasts. And yet it does exist. It must; hundreds have sacrificed their lives in pursuit of it over the centuries.

To mark the first time St. Augustine of Hippo set foot on the shores of this island, a coin was constructed of such elongatedness that some say it stretched right round the world. This slender means of exchange, this monetary girdle, was buried somewhere, at some point in the century when Chaucer topped the Sunday Times Bestseller list. No one knows where. An elite corp of the Elongated Society is devoted to its discovery. Dubbed the Knights of the Elongated Coin, few have even met them. Some say they meet in various gentlemen's clubs in Whitehall every few years to dine privately and pool their findings. Others say... well, let us leave what others might say. I don't care what they say.

If you are thinking to yourself, "I have never seen an elongated coin," and feel that your life is the worse for it, do not fret. Stay calm. There may come a day when, at one of those awful machines in a car-park which refuses to take your pound coin, you may find yourself in luck. Stop your cursing and your kicking, cease your muttered threats to burn the town hall to the ground.

Cast your eyes south to the coin in your hand.

It may very well be elongated.

The Regents Park Labour Party

Owls and a Blackbird lending feathered support to the Suffragist Movement

Along with thousands of others I am occasionally wont to guide my weary footsteps park-ward. Sick and dizzy with the fumes of London's roads, mind throbbing with high-finance and important business decisions of the hour, it is pleasant to imbibe, for an hour or so, the cool green waters of Regent's Park.

As one strolls past the peaceful glistening lake and the boating concession, the bandstand and the rose-gardens; as one leans distractedly over the little footbridge and casts a benign eye upon the various water-birds below – upon none of whom can one bestow accurate names but who are for all that no less beautiful - as one smiles at the other examples of friendly wildlife gambolling secretly amongst the willows and the oleanders, then widens ones gaze to embrace the expansive lawns and meadows beyond, stretching all the way up to the Zoo; as one feasts ones' soul upon all these visions of peace and contentment, it is with some surprise that one learns that Regents Park has its own branch of the Labour Party.

Yes. That's right. This 472 acre demi-paradise, this green jewel set in a concrete sea, this – well, you get the picture – this place has its own need for a socialist political force?

Why? How? One pictures in the early days of Labour Kier Hardie wandering through the park – perhaps taking a break from speaking in Trafalgar Square – and thinking to himself – "Yes! I will bring social justice even to this duck-pond! These mallards – ignorant, feathered fools that they are – will one day bask in proletarian bliss, content in the knowledge that they now own the means of production, distribution and exchange!"

Did Marx's vision of egalitarianism extend to plant and animal life? Are the shrubs victims of exploitation? Are the roses lording it over the weeds? Did he envisage liberation for legumes? What need, in short, has a vast expanse of greenery and tame fauna for political ideology –

an ideology, indeed, of the oppressed, the revolutionary, the egalitarian?

How can a squirrel own the means of production? He relies on the tree for nuts, I suppose. Does he therefore have the right to take over the tree, topple him from his position of woody power and henceforth take charge of all protein production? How can this be achieved? Is this why Regents Park has its own branch of the Labour Party?

Would one trust a kingfisher with the banking system? I would have grave doubts should I enter my local branch, sail breezily up to the cash-desk only to see a beak resting on the counter. And as for a muntjack, I would seriously hesitate before conferring upon him the role of Chancellor. The whole thing smacks of recklessness.

And yet I say it again: Regent's Park has its own branch of the Labour Party. Yes, I know, there are people living *round* the park – but let's be honest, the houses are so palatial the odds are pretty slim that anyone who lives there is going to be a confirmed socialist. Hardened Tories maybe. So Labour gets the park.

Can animals be socialist? Can they exhibit altruistic behaviour? Wolves, I am told, wait for the pack to catch up in order to share a meal. But there are no wolves in Regents Park. At least, that's what I've been told. Do birds distribute wealth? Only in worm-form, and only to their offspring. Their altruism does not extend beyond their own immediate family.

Yet I like the idea that Regents Park has its own branch of the Labour Party. I wonder what the turnout is at elections? I've never seen chaffinches queuing up at the polling booth. Perhaps they have their own special booths in the park, nailed to trees.

Or maybe the residents of the Zoo form the bulk of its membership? That is perhaps a more realistic suggestion – for as caged beasts they may be suffering a few social grievances. Size of meals, visitation rights etc. Perhaps the founding fathers of the Labour Movement envisaged an uprising of imprisoned animals, beasts breaking out of cages, sundering bars, vaulting fences, and executing their keepers like so many Antoinettes.

They haven't broken out yet. Perhaps they're not Labour. Maybe Regents Park has its own branch of the Conservative Party, which has won over the occupants of ZFL, or whatever flashy acronym it's known by today. Animals are, indeed, a notoriously conservative bunch. They don't like change. That must be it. I wonder what Kier Hardie can have been thinking of in the first place, setting up a branch of the Labour Party in the park. He was on a hiding to nothing. Hadn't he heard the expression "Animal Kingdom?" The clue's in the name. Animals are feudal, and there's an end to it.

The Free George Davis Society

As a gawky youth I became dimly aware on the fringes of my consciousness of a strange artist at work in the suburbs wherein I dwelt. Like the outpourings of some 1970's single-issue Banksy, though artistically cruder, on walls, railway bridges, outside sports grounds, several mysterious words began to appear, daubed in white paint. It was a simple message. It never varied.

It consisted of three simple words: *"Free George Davis."* True, sometimes it said "Fred George Davis." I began to muse that "Fred George Davis" could be some wholly separate organisation, whose aims were merely to advertise the existence of said Mr. D. Either that or a slip of the paintbrush.

Being young and foolish and with other things on my mind I didn't trouble myself to find out who or what George Davis was. The only thing I knew was that someone wanted him free. But from what? A sense of regret? A cardigan snagged on a nail? His illusions? As the graffiti spread, - here on a motorway bridge, here on a garden wall - so the figure of George Davis began to assume mythical proportions in my mind, like some kind of Prometheus chained to a rock by Zeus. Free him, by God, all Davis did was to provide man with fire!

The Society soon moved from paint to protest, slogan to streaking. It was clearly not enough simply to write their protests on various municipal brick walls, they also felt compelled to show us their genitals at various sporting fixtures. Or am I incorrectly mixing up mere motiveless streaking with the George Davis campaign? Their chronological proximity in the 1970's perhaps is the cause of this confusion. News reports in that heady decade seemed to contain little else but items on the continuing campaign to liberate Mr. D. and naked men running across cricket pitches. Nothing else happened, apart from a heat wave and everyone having to play scrabble by candlelight. Did members of the Free George

Davis campaign use streaking as part of their PR? I cannot swear.

Mr. Davis had been a petty crook who had been banged up wrongly for a crime he hadn't committed, of that we were all certain. Plenty of people were telling us so. He had committed many other crimes, but no one spoke about them. On 4th April 1974 a robbery took place at the London Electricity Board, Ilford. Do electricity boards keep the money we give them on the premises? I find that hard to believe. Nevertheless, their offices were robbed, and George Davis most emphatically was nowhere near the place. Of that we are certain. The Free George Davis Campaign told us so.

And yet the following year, in March 1975, he was convicted. His friends were outraged. And so they should be. He didn't do it. It didn't matter that he'd done loads of other crimes. Oh no. He did not do the *Ilford Electricity Board* job.

Celebrities rallied to his cause. Roger Daltrey of The Who sang about him; Bishops pleaded on local news programmes, activists wept in the streets. The 1970's was a golden age of radical groups; organisations with so many letters in their names the cost of their stationery must have been astronomical took up the cause of the East End villain. Even the Angry Brigade got involved at one point. Mind you, they got tetchy about practically everything.

One person who suffered at the hands of the Free George Davis Campaign was a chap called

George Ince. He had his own campaign: the Free George Ince Campaign. It never took off like Davis'. No one sang about George Ince in the pop charts. I don't think Roger Daltrey had even heard of him. There may have been a few slogans painted on railway bridges, but they didn't last long. The campaigners must have used an inferior paint. I'm sure also that several of the more indolent members of the George Davis Campaign must have arrived, paint-pot in hand, at a railway bridge, spotted the rival message, and simply crossed out the "Ince" and replaced it with a "Davis." It was a happy co-incidence that both were called George. It strikes me in hindsight that the two campaigns would have done well to pool their labour and resources. A better slogan might have been "Free the Georges Davis & Ince." Once liberated they could perhaps have formed a double-act, "Davis & Ince" and sung comic songs in working men's clubs.

But all the singing and all the marching and all the painting paid off, for in May 1976 the Home Secretary Roy Jenkins released George Davis. I believe he may have been pressured by representatives of the Department of Public Works, who feared the country would run out of paint. Whatever the reason, Mr. Davis was a free man.

And that would have been the end of the Free George Davis Campaign, were it not for the fact that not long after he was freed he was put in prison again.

How ungrateful. It's as if eight weeks after Nelson Mandela were released he promptly went and robbed a post office in Pretoria. It would have been plain rude.

After his second imprisonment the Free George Davis Campaign showed a natural reluctance to revive their activities. Paintbrushes remained dried and unused in petty crook's garages across the suburbs.

The original slogans became sad and faded. I'm sure there were plenty of people around who wanted him free again. But they stayed in their homes, and confided their hopes privately amongst friends and relatives over tea. Rumour has it that a campaign started that called itself "Don't bother freeing George Davis," but these rumours are unfounded.

Today, George Davis is once again free, and living a blameless life in his beloved Essex. Even as recent as May 2011 he was still fighting in the courts to prove his innocence over the LEB robbery some thirty-five years earlier. And the Judge did pronounce the conviction unsafe, though refused to completely exonerate him.

I admire Davis' perseverance, but it is a bit like Goering at Nuremberg confessing to every crime in the book whilst being incandescent with rage that he's been accused of jay-walking. Then devoting the rest of his life to expunging that one misdemeanour from his roll-call of aberrations. What is more, the eagerness with which every radical group in London rushed to the assistance of a known armed robber also sticks in the craw somewhat. It's not as though Davis was a heroic freedom fighter, a Che Guevara of Barking – he was a thug who used weapons in his crimes and who was revving up the getaway car when a man was clubbed to the floor nearby.

But I cannot help wondering if he ever catches the train into Marylebone Station and, casting a baleful eye at the sidings, spots a strange fading sign still clinging stubbornly to the tunnel wall; and, a lump forming in his throat, leans back and - eyes glazed - thinks back fondly on the days when, it seemed, the whole world wanted him free.

The United Kingdom Lubricants Association

In 2005, deep in the heart of Berkhamstead, a fierce war was being waged between various power-groups in the bitterly competitive world of lubrication. Its result was the United Kingdom Lubricants Association. Its birth was difficult. Many lives were lost in its cause. The war was fought between the BLF (the British Lubicrants Federation), and the UK Delegation to the UEIL. You will not read about this war in the history books, though its campaigns were just as bloody and bitter.

The origin of the dispute? Like the First World War, its beginnings are lost in the tangled mists of time. Suffice to say that at bottom lurked the ugly demonic need for power. You had on the one hand the plucky Tommies of the BLF, united in their love of lubrication, and on the other, the UEIL, with their pan-European ambitions and their desire to lubricate the entire continent. It seemed that moistening these islands was not enough for them – no, they wanted more. Jealous of the UEIL's territorial ambitions the BLF held secret meetings above snooker halls in Berkhamstead. Maps were unfurled, plots were hatched. A newsletter was released – the BLF would be marching into Europe too.

The killing started. Members of the UEIL were found drowned in vats of lubricant on various wastelands up and down southern Herts. Eager young infantrymen of the BLF were martyred with their own oil-based chemical compounds. Lubricators' widows were a common sight in the Home Counties, laying flowers beneath stone monuments. A huge mausoleum was built in Letchworth in the shape of a giant can of 3-in-one.

This madness continued for six long months. It had to stop. One sane voice rose up from the crowd: *"Unite or die!"* Weapons were lowered. Peace talks were held. Generals of the Lubrication world shook hands, embraced, wept. Maps were furled up again, military campaigns abandoned. An independent group – it matters not what their name was, only that they talked of peace and justice – arbitrated long into the night. As dawn broke over Berkhamstead the lubricating guns fell silent. The church bells rang. The United Kingdom Lubrication Association was born.

For generations to come the sons and grandsons of lubricators will be told this tale as they bounce on oily overalled knees. "Tell us about the Great Merger of 2005!" they will pipe up. And they will be told, and their eyes will mist over with pride.

It is a salutary tale, and one which the rival parties in the Middle East might well benefit from. Perhaps we could replace the current Peace envoy to that tragic region – a Mr. Blair I believe – with the current chairperson of the UKLA. He could sit down with the leader of Hamas and the Prime Minister of Israel and say, "listen chaps. You don't need to speak to me of conflict. I've seen it all. Rivalry in the lubrication business is every bit as deadly as your five thousand year old problem here. We were bickering about different ways of organising the lubricant industry when you were little Arabic nippers paddling in the Red Sea. Leave it to us. We will – literally – pour oil on troubled waters."

It could work. I must make a 'phone call.

The Society of Hotel Bed Jumpers

Seldom have I encountered a Society with a more specific aim, quite frankly. They are not just bed jumpers, no – they are hotel bed jumpers. And yet, a minute's musing on the logistics of this club raises some pretty penetrating questions. They call themselves a Society – and a worldwide one at that – and yet the very act of jumping on a hotel bed can be best achieved, surely, in a solitary manner? Surely a better title for their organisation would be: a "Large Group of People Scattered around the Globe, each of whom enjoy the occasional bounce on a bed in a Guest House of varying sizes from Bed and Breakfast to five-star hotel, but who never actually get together to participate in collective undertakings of said mattress-based elevation."

But of course that would be ridiculous. The cost of their letterheads would be prohibitive.

It might be more fun if they did get together. After all, some of the fondest memories of our entire lives must surely be reducing our beds to state of miserable, creaking suffering by five of us at least – not forgetting the boy from across the road who we didn't even invite but who keeps coming round anyway – jumping like lunatics up and down, up and down, until a Mother's screams brings our unfettered delight to a kill-joy end and we slink off sullen into the garden.

Is every hotel in the world a fit venue for the practices of this organisation? There is nothing in the Society's archives that suggest that some are out of bounds. I'd like to witness such a spectacle at the Savoy or the Dorchester. The look on the face of the room-service waiter would be a treat. He wheels in dinner, whisks off the silver cloche with a "voila!" – only be pulled up sharply by the sight of the middle-aged couple enjoying a pre-meal trampolining on the four-poster.

Does the Society have any notable members? Rumours circulate that the late Duke and Duchess of Argyll were avid enthusiasts. It got so that their names began appearing on hotel blacklists for fear that said establishments would lose a fortune in mattresses. Certain Prime Ministers and Monarchs, too, are suspected to be members - under assumed names of course. There was a famous occasion when at the Four Seasons in Rome after a certain G2 Summit staff were shocked to discover a bed in the penthouse suite in such a deplorable condition that it had to be re-sprung. It would not be slanderous of me to utter two simple words: Angela Merkel.

Are there any rules to this sport? May I call it a sport? Thank you. The answer in short is no, for rules would necessitate a referee and in certain establishments of course no guests are permitted after ten o'clock. I am thinking of Mrs. Nuttall's bed and breakfast in Queens Road Brighton. You know who you are.

There are, however, some members of this society who have apparently begun to take it all a little too seriously, and whose take on the pursuit has moved from viewing it as a harmless recreational activity to a fiercely competitive activity. I am talking of course of the notorious Hotel Bed-Jumping World Record Attempt of 2007. It took place at the White Horse Hotel, Marlborough, on August 15th. Six teams took part, overrunning the entire establishment. The building was crammed with referees, linesmen, eiderdown-straighteners, trainers, managers, timekeepers – the whole thing got slightly out of hand. Bob and Rita Lansbury won – I think the figures were two thousand and eight bounces in an hour. But the record attempt itself was overshadowed by the aftermath, in which the Berkshire Constabulary figured as prominent actors. Pyjama-clad bed-jumpers were pursued through revolving doors, couples were arrested mid-flight in Honeymoon suites, and timekeepers were wrestled to the ground by sous-chefs. Such was the chaos that the record itself was never formally recorded. Luckily Bob and Rita Lansbury's sentence was not custodial. They were released with a severe caution, and lived to bounce another day. I say luckily, for their propensity for bed-jumping could have got them into the little spot of bother in E Block of Strangeways. Knuckles Golightly likes his beauty sleep. He wouldn't have appreciated someone jumping up and down on the top bunk.

So next time you're enjoying a quiet weekend at the Rose Vista, Littlehampton and are disturbed by a regular brassy creaking from the room above – do not fold the pillow around your ears in politeness. Listen in awe. Count the bounces if you wish. But please don't call the police. It may be Bob and Rita making another record attempt.

The Made Up Textiles Association

Upon learning of the existence of this august group an image sprang to mind of a clandestine club of daydreamers who, disillusioned with the finite number of textiles in this world, decided to meet once a month and exchange ideas for cloths that have never, nor will ever, or *can* ever, be actually made. This cadre of Fabric-Fantasists, these Poets of Polyester, this happy band devoted to whimsical wefts and weaves, would sit in secret rooms above pubs and spin yarns about yarn and converse long into the evening about cloth that would and could never exist.

They might well be a surreal and more experimental offshoot of the Textile Society, a bit like the Post-Impressionists following the Impressionists. Several whippersnappers at a Textile Society Meeting perhaps stood up one day and, fists thumping on tables, cried out "Stop mentioning real textiles! Tell us something we don't know!" – and stormed off to invent their own manifesto. These Dadaists of the realm of cloth then presented to the world their findings: tapestries woven from the frozen tears of a thousand dwarves; scarves made of wood; glass dresses, hats made of regret and shoes stitched from the dreams of a shy nursemaid. The creative output of such a society is of course infinite.

Their patron saint would of course be the two tailors from "The Emperor's New Clothes," immortalised in a painting on their clubhouse wall. The more realisable of their made-up textiles would be worn by the individual responsible to their monthly meetings. Owl-feather socks, perhaps, or honey pyjamas.

Lady Gaga's flair for sartorial whimsicality would doubtless ensure an invitation to become Honorary President. Followed perhaps by a guest visit with her husband Lord Gaga – a certainty for the front cover of the next "Made Up Textile Society Quarterly."

The Made Up Textile Association is always on the look-out for new members. Fancy joining? It's easy. Just think of your own fabric. Make it as ridiculous as possible. Done it? Good. You're in. Write to them at 16, Bellington Close, Hitchin, Herts HT9 OBW. And if you write your letter on the skin of a unicorn, they'll probably knock off your first years' subscription.

The Esperance Club

One of my favourite Societies in this volume, the Esperance Club was born in the late nineteenth century as a manifestation of that wonderful wave of altruism and compassion that lifts the Victorian Age well above our own. Compared to our state-run, state-administered welfare machine, the Victorians, with their active voluntary charity, their muscular Christianity and their individual philanthropy, gave themselves a sense of spiritual uplift simply unattainable by the act of slowly, painfully, paying an income tax bill.

Some of the Victorian solutions to working-class suffering were noble – compulsory education, free libraries etc. Others were a little more eccentric. Like the Esperance Club.

Founded in the mid 1890's by Emmeline Pethwick-Lawrence and Mary Neal, the aims of the club were to alleviate the distress being experienced by young female dressmakers in London. The industry was long-known for its hardship and its reduction of "happy, healthy women of the countryside" to a life of semi-starvation and struggle in the big city. Their plight was so well-advertised that Thomas Hood even wrote a poem about them:

Song of the shirt

With fingers weary and worn,
With eyelids heavy and red,
A woman sat, in unwomanly rags,
Plying her needle and thread –
Stitch! Stitch! Stitch
In poverty, hunger, and dirt,
And still with a voice of dolorous pitch
She sang the song "The Song of the Shirt.

How to help them? Well, in the 1890's Emmeline Pethwick-Lawrence and Mary Neal thought they had the answer. To alleviate the awful lives of working-class, lower middle-class and even middle-class women of a back-breaking often twenty-hour day in a back-room stitching endless dresses in poor light – they would... they would... I can hardly say this... they would teach them Morris Dancing.

Now, I've done my fair share of manual labour in my time - building-site labouring, kitchen-portering, the usual shenanigans one gets up to when one foolishly says to oneself aged about twenty that one will "pursue an acting career or perish." True, I have never sat in a dingy room in Aldgate and made twenty dresses for rich women in Knightsbridge for a couple of shillings a year. But, I can't help thinking that after a long shift lugging paving stones around, the last thing I'd want to do is to wash the brick-dust off my face, dress up in a red and green outfit with bells hanging from my hat, and go Morris-dancing.

Did Ms. Pethwick-Lawrence and Ms. Neal think this thing through? History does not record the response of the early members when, working-clothes discarded, they were ushered into some obscure dance-hall in St. Pancras, London, presented with costumes, and instructed in the art of hopping back and forth whilst hitting eachother with little sticks? One imagines it ran along the lines of "This madness must stop. And stop at once," or "Ms. Pethwick-Lawrence, thank you ever so much for thinking of me, but please – I don't want to do this dancing. It is not alleviating my suffering."

Ethel Carstairs bravely ignoring her hunger pangs and launching into her fourth hour of Fol-de-Rol.

Maybe I'm being churlish, but wouldn't it have been better to sell the Morris-dancing costumes and give the girls the money? Perhaps not.

Perhaps the girls thoroughly enjoyed themselves: a brief terpsichorean interlude between long bouts of drudgery never hurt anyone. Indeed, it is probably a fair description of everyone's lives.

Socialist Party of England & Wales (SPEW)

Formed as an offshoot of the Militant Tendency in 1964, SPEW finds itself in this volume for frankly crude yet obvious reasons. On what particular evening in a smoke-filled room above a pub in Hackney this acronymic nightmare of an association came to be is not known. One thing is certain - they were surely drunk at the time.

My reasoning is simple. If you are intending to form a breakaway party with the aim of better representing the radical views of the populace of Wales and England, it might be politely suggested that you not plump for a name whose initials indicate one of the less pleasant biological functions?

Perhaps I am being harsh. Perhaps if I were at the meeting I would have come up with something equally ridiculous. Perhaps the meeting went on late into the night. A lot of alcohol had doubtless been consumed and acronyms were probably flying about like some kind of weird flock of alphabetic birds. So many perhapses and so few answers!

At the beginning of the meeting I'm sure a few sensible suggestions were made. But as the night wore on the suggestions clearly worsened. To end with SPEW as the best one, one shudders at what some of the previous ones were. Maybe the minds of the committee were so fogged that by two o'clock in the morning when some rum cove mumbled "SPEW" they accepted it without a murmur. Indeed, they probably cheered.

The aim of SPEW, as far as I can make out, was to distance itself from the Militant Tendency, another organisation with whose name I have several doubts. I've always felt the word *tendency* smacks of a certain weakness. Did Lenin call his noble revolutionary party the *Communist Inclination?* While most political societies want to make themselves sound as powerful or representative as possible, the addition of the word *tendency* seems to lend the title a distinct sense of self-undermining. As if its members are saying, "Look, we're radical okay? We're definitely radical. But we want you know that we just kind of *lean* towards radicalism. We don't want to go the whole way – God forbid. We wish to simply edge ourselves, slowly and gradually and sensibly, towards a militant stance. We're not even sure if we are going to be militant about everything. No. We may very well take a liberal, kind-hearted view of a lot of things. We'll let you know. Don't pressure us. Go away."

And so SPEW was born. One envisages the morning after. One sees the piled up ashtrays, the overturned glasses. A befugged and dry-mouthed member – let us call him Sid - lifts his head from a sticky beermat.

The full horror slowly dawns. Tim the Assistant Secretary comes in with a pile of new letter-head freshly printed. He hands them round proudly.

"Wha...?" Sid can hardly speak.

A dozen hardened English and Welsh Socialists read, and gulp.

"What have we done? SPEW?? You flipping idiot, Tim."

"But you said ," –

"Never mind what we said! Are you sure we settled on SPEW?"

"We can always change it."

"How many have we had printed?"

"Twenty thousand."

There follows a pregnant pause as lengthy as the gestation period of the elephant.

"SPEW it is."

So they were stuck with it. They'd printed the leaflets. And they are still stuck with it, for it still exists.

The Fairy Investigation Society

I recall as a youngster that the existence of fairies was a given, their veracity unchallengeable. After all, you could see them everywhere, especially in summer. They weren't thistledown. Oh no. They were fairies. I had it on good authority. Denis Baker told me. He once tried to catch one. It was a late Spring morning and three of us were ambling down a lane near where we lived to a field, where we were going to idle away a day. A fairy came floating by. Our hearts quickened.

"Kill it!" commanded Denis Baker, and he was off.

Just then a gentle breeze came up and took the fairy out of his reach, so thankfully he didn't execute the sprite. But I recall this event primarily because I remember distinctly believing with my whole heart and soul that this aery little piece of fluffy thistledown was indeed a being from another realm, one of the little people, an elf of the air, a naiad.

Sadly my belief died. Others were not so unfortunate, and I envy them. I envy every member of the Fairy Investigation Society.

Founded in 1927 by Sir Quentin Crauford to catalogue fairy sightings, the Society flourished right up until the Second World War, when the chaos scattered members across the globe and drove the organisation into semi-oblivion. After all, when V1s are crashing all around you the last thing on your mind, quite frankly, is "I wonder if I'll see a pixie today?"

But in 1955 it re-ignited itself, and went on a recruiting drive. Its membership rose to include such notables as the writer Alisdair Alpine MacGregor, and even Walt Disney. More recently, it has dwindled in force and has moved across the Irish Sea to Dublin – home, perhaps, of a more persistent acceptance of faery lore.

The early twentieth century was a crucible of experimental spirituality tinged with mysticism: from Madam Blavatsky and her "wicked pack of cards," to the Society for Psychical Research," (See page....) to Rosicrucianism, Rudolf Steiner and Eastern influences. People, it seemed, were hungry for an expansion of consciousness beyond the flat and the everyday. Angels were sighted on the battlefield of Mons, respected pillars of rational literary society like Conan Doyle wrote persuasively on the existence of spirits, life after death, and indeed, fairies. They say the 1960's was a radical, explosive decade – but the seeds of the mystical outpourings of that time were sown in the years 1890-1950. And the Fairy Investigation Society was but one rivulet of that outpouring.

The story of the Cottingley Phenomena is well-known and has been exhaustively catalogued elsewhere, so I will not touch on those two mischievous sisters whose wonderful story and photographs sadly ended just that – a story.

Horace Winterbottom's faithful depiction of an encounter he had in a London garden, entitled 'What I saw on the night of August 3ʳᵈ 1910, and I'll fight anyone who says I'm lying.'

Disney's mysticism is well-known, but among the more surprising member of the Society was Air Chief Marshall Hugh Dowding. I say surprisingly only because the high level in society this head of the air arm occupied lends one to assume – perhaps wrongly - a certain "sensibleness." But what is sensibleness? He did his job. One can be grateful, of course, that his belief in the little people didn't distract him from the more pressing responsibilities that were weighing on his shoulders at the time, i.e. defending these islands against Adolf. One conjures a scene in the MOD of a trepidatious officer eagerly awaiting a decision on whether to deploy a squadron of fighter planes on the East coast or the West Coast - and a crazed Dowding on his knees on the floor babbling "The Goblins are coming! The Goblins are coming!" One is fairly sure such a scenario never took place.

The Semi-Colon Appreciation Society

If one was forced at gunpoint to prioritise ones charitable causes - not the likeliest of scenarios but there are some strange people about - I think most people would agree with me when I say the plight of the baby seal would probably figure slightly higher on ones' list than the fate of a small piece of punctuation humans call the 'semi-colon.' Indeed, many things would probably feature higher on ones list than the plight of the semi-colon. I'm not even sure that the semi-colon has a 'plight.' Can punctuation suffer? It certainly suffers at the hands of texters. Yet this is not suffering in the sense of it possessing a nervous system and therefore feeling pain whenever it is left out, mangled or misused. I have never seen a question mark weep. A forward slash cannot be bruised.

That the semi-colon is in decline there is no doubt. For some years now it has had a deadly foe, and that deadly foe has been the comma. Like the battle between the Red Squirrel and the Grey Squirrel the comma has driven the semi-colon out of its natural habitats across Europe, destroyed its nests, and chased its young through the woods of sentences across the continent. One might describe this conquering as a kind of 'punctuational cleansing.' One is almost moved to contact the European Court of Human Rights, Linguistic Division.

At first glance it seems quite strange to think that the comma should be victorious over the semi-colon. It is smaller for a start. After all, what is a comma but a dotless semi-colon? It's as if a race of midgets were to rise up and vanquish all tall people. Or people without hats drive people with hats out of the town. Yet it has won. And the reason it has won is probably for that very reason; in our ever-accelerating society it is easier to dash off a comma than a semi-colon. Although – and this is a big although – with electronic communicating outstripping handwriting tenfold these days, it is just as easy to dash off a semi-colon on ones keypad. So that puts the kybosh on that argument. I'm sorry I mentioned it.

I'm with Stephen Fry when it comes to grammar. Let it be. There is no right use of grammar. Language is an untrammelled beast, wild and free, roaming throughout the real world, not to be fossilized and observed in a remote study. It is an ever-changing thing, a chimera, a chameleon, a shifting pebbled beach. Trying to enforce grammatical rules is akin to Canute attempting to force back the waves. One might as well try to legislate against erosion.

I like the semi-colon. But if it is to die, let us give it a decent burial. After all, if language and grammar had not changed over the centuries, then we would still be grunting and squeaking for our supper. Some might say that in certain fast-food outlets we still do. But that is another question.

The Arctic Morris Dancing Group of Helsinki

One should be proud, I suppose, that our only native English folk dance is a big hit in the Arctic Circle, and has a branch there. After all, who of us, when wandering a foreign capital, does not experience a small frisson of pride when spotting a Marks & Spencer?

Morris Dancing is an odd pursuit at the best of times but a hobby even stranger when conducted - willingly - in sub-zero temperatures. Perhaps they have their own Arctic version of the costume made from thick gabardine with fur edged collars. Perhaps they utilise their environment and use icicles instead of wooden sticks.

I'd like to see a demonstration of Morris Dancing in Finland. But I have to confess I'd secretly be waiting to see one of them fall through the ice. There is a lot of hopping up and down in Morris Dancing, and there's a lot of ice in Finland. Perhaps the recreation could become a competitive sport, with the person remaining on top of the ice the winner. I'm not saying we should leave the losers to an icily watery fate.

Clearly there would be lifeguards on hand. I'm just saying that if such jeopardy was added to Morris Dancing, it would add a certain frisson to the spectacle.

Jeopardy should be introduced to the English version too. I mean jeopardy beyond the possibility of being hit accidentally on the wrist with a small stick. There should be Morris Dancing through hoops of fire perhaps. Or motorcycle Morris, where the participants bob and weave amongst each other driving their metallic steed single-handedly whilst bashing each other with batons.

I suppose one should be very proud that this – albeit odd – aspect of English culture is being celebrated abroad. The Japanese have many thriving Sherlock Holmes societies. I am told – though this is unproven – that erstwhile star of ITV sitcom "On the Buses" Reg Varney is worshipped as a god in remote Venezuelan villages. So the Finnish adopting our most folkish of terpsichorean antics is not something to be mocked. Along with Harry Potter, James Bond and Stilton cheese, we must celebrate it as a successful export. I'm not sure it is worth as many billions to our coffers than Rowling's tales of whimsical wizardry, but it's something.

So if you find yourself in Finland, and see a group of men and women in green and red hopping about on the ice and hitting each other with sticks, do not call a Doctor. It is not a hallucination brought on by the snow. It is a long-reaching tentacle of this sceptred isle reaching out across the North Sea and tickling the fancy of our cold, but happy cousins.

The Telegraph Pole Appreciation Society

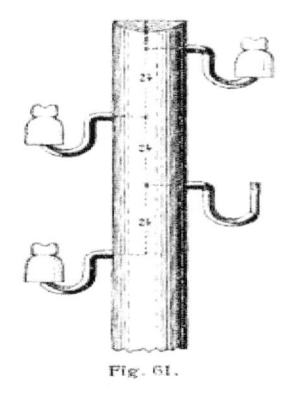

Fig. 61.

I have no problem with the bare fact that telegraph poles can be appreciated – the very thought. My problem with this august group of odd-fellows is - *how* does one show appreciation to a telegraph pole? I'm not sure it would return a love-letter. And I'm convinced it would not like being stroked. A certain gaze of admiration as one passes by in a car, yes. Maybe that's all that's needed. Perhaps a wave. A blown kiss. It was once a tree, so maybe a hug would suffice.

Over the centuries we have bent the tree to our will. When once we lived in its branches and ate its leaves, we now chop it down and make it into sofas. And upon the invention of the telegraph and the telephone, what better way to drape the infinite cables across our countries and continents than by stitching them from fake treetop to fake treetop.

The Telegraph Appreciation Society might never have existed. A dreadful thought I am sure you'll agree. For in the mid-nineteenth century Samuel Morse himself intended the cables to be buried underground. Luckily, so many faults occurred with this method that the only solution was to build those odd regimented forests which now criss-cross our nations like so many giant cribbage pegs, its buzzing and crackling wires hung between them like dangerous evil versions of a million washing-lines. The world's first telegraph poles were born from a single advertisement placed by Morse in a Washington newspaper on February 7th 1844: "Sealed proposals will be received by the undersigned for furnishing 700 straight and sound chestnut posts with the bark on and of the following dimensions to wit: Each post must not be less than eight inches in diameter at the butt and tapering to five or six inches at the top. Six hundred and eighty of said posts to be 24 feet in length, and 20 of them 30 feet in length."

Some of these chestnut pioneers and their pine protégées served their country well for eighty years. The telegraph pole has a long working-life. They are rarely retired off to eke out a miserable recycled existence as a park bench or a Christmas log. Through bitter winters and blisteringly hot summers they stand proud, carrying our voices night and day across city and wilderness. No wonder they have an appreciation society – in fact I am thinking of joining it myself.

From 'The Vandalism Must Stop!'
- a Telegraph Pole Appreciation Society
Publication by Alan Strang

They have their enemies of course. The anti-Visual Polluters. These reprobates claim that any scarring of the skyline is a form of optical poison. The fools. Can they not see the beauty in the serried ranks of smoothed and leafless trees that wear their wires like widows weeds, in dignity, and selflessness? No, I am firmly in the telegraph pole camp. I will defend them to my dying breath.

If any of you wish to join the society, it will cost you a measly fifteen pounds. This is a scant outlay when you consider the benefits you receive. For a start, there is the welcome pack. There's always a welcome pack. There's a welcome pack for everything. Even when you move house these days more often than not there is a welcome pack from the council lying on your new doormat. I bought a packet of nicotine gum the other day and found an (admittedly small) welcome pack in the box. 'Welcome to the wonderful world of chewable nicotine!' it declared.

As a tangential benefit, your fifteen pounds outlay may be returned to you tenfold for, as a member, you will have the opportunity to start collecting ceramic GPO insulators. Yes, you heard me correctly. These much south-after items of "telegraph-pole furniture" exchange for thousands at auctions up and down the country. They date from the days when the Post Office ran the telegraph poles. Indeed, the Post Office seemed to run everything. They even had their own huge tower in central London. Now the poles are managed by various conglomerates such as BT, NG, and other initial-identified companies who refuse to be known by anything other than an acronym.

But you can still buy a pole if you want. There's a company called "Total Poles" which, at a price, will deliver a pole to your door. The pole will have performed a lifetime's noble service, and will be looking for a new home. The company says, "a used pole has a multitude of uses." But it doesn't say exactly what. Caber-tossing? A very simple Christmas tree?

One might as well appreciate telegraph poles. They're not going to go away. Or are they? With wirelessness on the advance, who knows. Perhaps one day our landscapes will be pole-less. And then the members of their Appreciation Society will not be found in remote parts of the countryside with flasks of tea and cameras – but in museums, where bemused crowds will gather at the foot of a once-mighty totem, like so many supplicant pagans.

The Eccentric Club

The origins of this august and historic association lies way back in that delightful period of English history when the sole aim of female fashion seemed to be to worship the female cleavage to the point of idolatry: the age of coffee-houses and snuff, dandies, stagecoaches and toy theatres. 1781 is the officially recorded year of the club's foundation, though it has faded and reappeared in various guises periodically ever since. Over the years it has been known as the Illustrious Society of Eccentrics, the (optimistic beyond bravado) Everlasting Society of Eccentrics, the Eccentric Society Club (a result perhaps of a heated and unresolved debate between two hotly indignant camps) and – most oddly – the Eccentric Club Limited. Did the latter seek to manufacture eccentrics? Did some form of hideous factory exist, with a conveyor belt, breeding mavericks like so many battery hens?

Its latest incarnation is thriving at the London Arts Club in Dover Street, and has Prince Philip as its honorary President and Prince William the Duke of Cambridge as Honorary life Member. It has recently celebrated its 239th anniversary, and appears to be going from strength to strength.

Its original foundation as a society for "original thinkers and achievers" has perhaps been strayed from slightly like a forgetful rambler wandering, map-less and somewhat bewildered, from a footpath that peters out into woodland and pasture. Yet their aims seem pure. They celebrate complete political and religious impartiality ever since their acrimonious split from the Whig-dominated society, the (modestly) titled The Brilliants. Their mission statement, as gleaned from the declarations of their various previous incarnations, remains to foster "Nothing but Good," and to "Worship the Three Muses."

I'd like to have met some of the "Brilliants." They actually seem more eccentric than the Eccentrics. In fact, I think it's a truism to state that anyone who thinks of himself as eccentric, or describes themselves as eccentric, is probably not that eccentric. It's a bit like people who describe themselves as mad. "I'm mad, me!" No you're not. If you were actually mad you'd be lying tranquillised in a white hospital room. Jumping up and down in a nightclub and screaming is not being "mad," it's being utterly, expectably normal. Bringing an inflatable hammer to a party is also not being mad. Only people who don't think they are eccentric are eccentric – like every member of every other club in this book. If you Morris dance in Finland, you are eccentric. If you launch a space rocket from Pinner, you are eccentric. If you join a club called the Eccentric Club, you are not eccentric. I'm sorry, they are my rules, and I'm probably right.

Perhaps the Eccentric Club should rename themselves the "Needy People who want to Appear Different Club." A bitter pill to swallow, but probably true.

The Beetle Fight Club

When men are tired fighting each other, they move on to the next best thing – getting insects to fight each other. At bottom, humanity has a strain of squalid sadistic voyeurism about it, and in the case of Beetle Battling, as it is called, it is our hard-shelled six-legged cousins who bear the brunt of such base appetites.

In back streets and alleyways across the world, on obscure patches of waste-ground or in dimly-lit basements lit only by slowly swinging naked light-bulbs, leering crowds form grubby circles and press forward eagerly to catch a sweaty glimpse of 'their man', or, more accurately, 'their beetle.'

Beetles fight in the wild of course, so perhaps the above lurid moral outrage is a little invidious. Are men not simply harnessing the natural urges that pre-exist within the average red-blooded Stag Beetle? Probably. Maybe I just enjoyed writing about 'grubby circles pressing forward eagerly,' etc. One can get quite carried away with these things.

The Beetle Fight Club is perhaps the most notorious of these underground societies of insectivorous conflict, and is based in Thailand. For a small fee, and if you mix with the right chaps, you can inveigle your way into an underground bar with softly swaying lanterns, and a bar that wouldn't be out of place in the Old Kent Road, and witness some spellbinding bouts between beetles famed far and wide for their pugilistic prowess. Some fighters have become as famous as their human counterparts. 'Raging Beetle Hulahan' springs to mind – an insect who pulled himself up from the ghetto to punch and claw his way to a notoriety and fame across two hemispheres. Of course, he changed his name to 'Raging Mohammed' in the mid-sixties when he converted to Islam, and some say his filmed fight against Colin 'The Claw' Bootle was staged – but he'd clocked up enough noteworthy bouts in previous years to guarantee him a place in the Insect Manuals. Rumours abound that Martin Scorsese is planning a biopic of the legendary horned demi-god. Time will tell. I cannot say who will be playing him, but in recent months Robert de Niro has been spotted living underground in a series of tunnels below the Arizona desert and feeding on leaves and greenfly. Surely the Oscars beckon.

Other great pincered champions of the ring did not fare as well as Raging Mohammed. Chang 'Razor-hands' Coolidge bludgeoned his way to great wealth, only to be stamped on in a drugs incident in the mid-seventies. This Scarface of the Coleoptera community, this Mike Tyson of the world of being a small fighting thing, was a sad loss to the sport. But the sport of beetle battling is bigger than any of its stars. It'll be happening somewhere near you. Tonight. Probably.

The legendary Spuds O'Shaughnessy locking horns with his old rival Lucky-Boy Gonzales.

The Esperanto Society

Every language had to start somewhere. At some point in history there was a single person who, before all others, uttered the word "foot."

There was no committee involved in its formation – the enterprising chap just came right out and said it. That's confidence for you. He must have been met with the odd quizzical glance from his fellow homo erecti. "Eh?" they must have grunted, with a vein of primitive sarcasm. "I've hurt my foot," he responded, confidence growing by the minute. Met with such self-assurance, how could the others not acquiesce? Colleagues were called in from the hunting grounds – "Quick!" their friends cried, "Sidney's thought of a word for that – that thing on the end of our legs!" "No!" rejoindered their pals, dropping their jaws and their spears, and hot-footing it – or hot-something-it – back to camp.

At first sceptical, then intrigued, then sceptical again, their puzzlement soon turned to joy. Sidney was slapped on the back. They all probably chatted happily about feet until the fire went out.

So to invent a language from scratch in the twentieth century is not an insane idea in itself – for, as the above historical scenario demonstrates, all language was invented at some point. So the singular failure of Esperanto to fulfil its aim of becoming the one, global, universal lingua franca of all humanity, does not lie in the absurdity of its foundation. No. It perhaps lies in that thing comedians and horologists hold most dear in their trades – timing. The bare fact is, when Esperanto was first mooted, all of us had already got a language. Come on, chaps, this vale of tears is hard enough as it is without being asked to ditch our mother tongues and fill our already-overloaded bonces with Latinate neo-logisms. Do us a favour!

Doubtless their aims were pure. Noble even. The propensity of otherwise quite civilised ladies and gentlemen in the nineteenth and twentieth centuries to seek – seemingly at the drop of a hat – to tear each other limb from limb, led to an enterprising and peace-loving Pole called Dr. Zamenhof to invent a whole new way of misunderstanding each other. His motives were wonderful. Others chaps were scrabbling round too for a solution to man's perennial nastiness: politicians formed the League of Nations; Bertrand Russell and others founded the Peace Movement. Zamehof toiled at his lingo.

I am reliably informed that although Esperanto never caught on as the main or even secondary language of any country, it is officially recognised in France and indeed is the language of instruction of the Academy of Sciences in the Republic of San Marino. I would like to attend a lecture at the Academy of Science in San Marino. I would like to attend a lecture on Einstein's Special Theory of Relativity. I might understand it in Esperanto. For I don't understand it in English.

I've studied a bit of Esperanto. It looks like Italian to me. That's good, because I can speak Italian. In Esperanto, for example, the word "Family" is "Familio". This leads me to believe that most of us Europeans at any rate could probably speak Esperanto simply by tagging the odd light-hearted "o" to our words. We could bring it off. There is a growing body of Esperanto literature. A dedicated bod is even working on an Esperanto version of "Finnegan's Wake." The brave lad has been at it for thirty-two years. I understand he's still on page four. And in a rest home in Kent. There are an estimated two million Esperanto speakers in the world. I should like them to have their own country. Not because I don't like them. I've never met them. On the contrary, I think it would give their language the stamp of authority it lacks at present. On the other hand, it may foster that very sense of nationalism the Esperantists were seeking to abolish in the first place. In fact, it's a ridiculous notion. Forget I mentioned it. Sorry.

Yet even without their own territory the prospect of Esperantists going to war with other invented language societies is not in the realm of impossibility. I hope it never happens.

Members of the 15th International Esperanto Congress staging a mass walkout after a member was overhead speaking Swiss.

The 'I Will Quit Society' of Blandford Forum

The inaugural meeting of the above society is a day that has gone down in Blandford Forum's history. I will try and relate the events in as calmly and plainly a fashion as I can. I think it's pretty clear from the outset that their troubles began with their name. Had they named themselves simply "I will Quit," then perhaps the riots would never have happened.

Let me start at the beginning. A man named Henry Bedstock it was who dreamt up the name: an enthusiastic non-smoker, he'd given up after many years and had decided to share his triumph and advice with his fellow townsfolk. And so the Society was born. The town hall was booked, posters went up.

Come the night of February 8th 1998, and Henry was setting up his power-point when he was disturbed by raised voices coming from the front entrance. In short, the town hall was besieged by a motley crowd of several hundred, all of them apparently suffering under the delusion that Henry Bedstock was some kind of guru who was there to offer them a panacea to all society's ills by leading them out of civilisation altogether and to some happy commune somewhere, where they could eke out their days in anti-social bliss.

Young and old – mainly young – travellers, hippies, seekers of truth – they all wanted to quit society, and they wanted Henry Bedstock to lead them.

It took hours for Henry to convince them that he wasn't Somerset's equivalent of the Dalai Llama. He mounted a plinth outside the town hall and bellowed his message through a loudhailer.

"No!" he cried, "We are not here to quit society!"

But the mob were having none of it.

"Yes we are!" they replied – a simple rejoinder which stated their position quite succinctly and effectively they thought.

A local reporter later stated that it resembled a scene from 'Life of Brian.'

Eventually the printers were blamed. Albert Pottage & Sons were summoned from their beds to account for themselves; in particular, why they had spelt 'Society' with a small 's.' I will not relate precisely what their response was – suffice to say it involved inserting a certain poster into areas of Henry Bedstock's being that he scarcely knew existed.

The crowd dispersed into the night. For a few short hours Blandford Forum had almost lost a large portion of its citizens to the Alternative Society.

Few spoke of it much after that. Henry Bedstock abandoned his society. Some say he even took up smoking again. But several people talk softly in the snug bars of the alehouses of Somerset, of the night when Henry Carshalton Bedstock almost led three hundred of Blanford Forum's townsfolk off to a commune on Salisbury Plain, to a better world, to a better life.

The American Headache Society

I shouldn't laugh at this well-meaning organisation, but I'm going to. I would not like to attend one of their meetings. For a start it would probably be held in a darkened room. And in such twilit chaos – curtains drawn, blinds down - you may well stumble across someone you don't want to see. Like an ex-mistress, or your bank manager. And those you do want to see you probably wouldn't recognise. "Nigel? Is that you? Oh, sorry, I thought you were Nigel."

And the meetings themselves – once everyone's stopped bumping into furniture, crashing into tables, dropping notebooks etc – once all that myopic palaver has been got out of the way, surely everyone – given the remit of the society – would be, how shall I say, a tad *irritable?*

I know I'm irritable when I have a headache. The pleasures of the world are but a figment of other people's imaginations whenever I'm in the grip of a cracking bonce-burner. You can keep your positive thinking, your jovial bonhomie, when a cranial thumper strikes yours truly. All my natural easy-going charm flies out of the window; I become a surly Heathcliffe, or a Mr. Rochester growling from atop his horse. I don't own a horse, but if I did I guarantee you I would glower from the top of it.

I can never see the end of it. I can never imagine a time when I did *not* have a headache. You may think I have a very poor imagination. And I would agree with you. But my excuse is that I like to live in the present. And when I have a headache, that is the only present I can envisage – a sort of never-ending, eternal present, one involving me having a nagging pain behind the eyes and forehead until the Day of Judgement.

So imagine the speeches at the meetings of the American Headache Society: grumpy would scarcely be sufficient to describe them.

"Rodney will now outline the findings of the clinical trials last month in Wisconsin. Rodney? Where's Rodney? *Rodney!*"

"Madam Chairwoman, could you please keep your voice down, I've got a terrible headache."

"We've all got terrible headaches, that's why we're here you stupid git!"

"Well, really!"

"And anyway, my headache's worse than yours, so just put a sock in it will you? *Rodney!!*"

Someone puts their hand up and informs the meeting that the much sought-after Rodney has been unable to attend owing to the fact that he's got a headache. This sends the Chairwoman apoplectic.

"That's the very time he should be attending!" she bellows, causing several members in the front row to cover their ears. "He wouldn't be of any use to us without a headache, would he!"

This observation creates a ripple of applause from a group of her hardened supporters, until they are 'shushed' by the row in front.

Then all hell breaks loose. Members start comparing anecdotes about their respective bouts of head-suffering, each trying to outdo each other.

"I was once in bed for three months!"

"It's a pity you're not in bed now!"

The row rages for fifteen minutes, then Muriel starts crying and someone fetches a glass of water.

The highlight of the year for the American Headache society is their Annual trip. They have to choose very quiet places, of course. A Museum of Eiderdowns, perhaps, or the remote foothills of the Himalayas. Maybe the odd excursion to a Trappist monastery.

I'm not sure of the point of this society. I think headaches are here to stay, like stubbing toes. There's no cure to them. Aspirin or paracetemol seem to do the trick for most. I think the main point is, of course, to meet and chat. Softly. About their suffering. We all like to do that. It's the reason we love Doctor's waiting rooms. And when we can't go to the Doctors, the next best thing is to join something like the American Headache Society.

The Aetherius Society

The Aetherius Society used to be in the Fulham Road, West London. I know that because I used to live there, and would pass their shop-window on the way home. I say shop – they never actually sold anything, unless you count their esoteric knowledge about... Well, there's the rub.
In the window of the offices of this illustrious society there was a big poster of a man with what can only be described as a steel helmet on his head, and various beams being transmitted from space into the helmet's antennae. In felt pen next to this poster were written the words "Communicating with the Beyond – the Aetherius Society."

This enigmatic *mise-e-scene* – a change from the usual shop window displays I think you'll agree – exerted a powerful affect upon me. I would loiter for – well, two minutes tops – gazing at it and wondering if I should go in. I never went in. I feared that not only would I be taught how to communicate with the beyond, there would be a strong likelihood of me being despatched to the beyond. So I would shuffle my footsteps for a moment, then walk on, never the wiser.

There were a few pamphlets in the window, but they didn't teach me much. I should have gone in, ok, yes, I should have gone in, alright? But I didn't.

And now it's too late. Twenty years went by. And one day I found myself in the Fulham Road. So I wandered (as though compelled?) towards that part of the long street which once housed the offices of they who 'communicate with the beyond.'

They had gone. Perhaps they had not only communicated with the beyond but decided to go the whole hog and hot-foot it to the beyond. Perhaps they couldn't quite hear what the beyond was trying to say to them, so had to get closer. Whatever the reason, the place was now a children's shoe shop.

I lingered at the window. Was this *still* the Aetherius Society? Had they simply got fed up with talking to aliens and become a footwear retailer? Or perhaps the sale of small-scale pumps and wellingtons was a just a front for the continuation of their original activity: communicating with the – well, you know.

I went in. The poster of the man with a helmet and antennae on his head was gone. In its place was small podium on which stood a rack of training shoes. There was nothing about the store that said: "this may look like a shoe-shop, but in the back-room we are having conversations with the inhabitants of Venus." There were simply shoes. Lots of them.

An assistant engaged me in small talk about my needs. I did not need a pair of children's shoes. I needed to know if she was Venusian. I didn't ask if she was a Venusian. She didn't look Venusian. She wasn't Venusian.

I will perhaps never find out what the true aims and achievements of the Eletheuria Society are. If anyone out there knows, please get in touch.

By the normal means, please. A letter, or fax will suffice. I don't want any voices in my head. I've enough of those.

This never happened in the Fulham Road.

The British Christmas Tree Growers Federation

I love Christmas trees. To this day my favourite smell is that of a freshly cut Christmas fir perhaps dragged through a slight dusting of snow along a village street, then set up, sparkling, in the corner of a living-room, preferably with some firelight reflected in a child's eyes. And Bing Crosby playing on the radiogram.

So please don't think I'm mocking these chaps. Yet once again I home in (quite ruthlessly, I know; I can be ruthless if the necessity arises) on the very pointedness of having to have an *association* in the first place? Why not just grow the things yourself without the need for banding together in some kind of tree-based tribal huddle?

We humans are obsessed with huddles. Everything has an association. Even shops. If we buy our goods at a certain store we're invited to join a 'Tesco's Club,' - with its own card of course. I scribble nonsense for a living, alone in a garret, and yet I am still invited on a weekly basis to join numerous organisations all of which assure me that I will be immeasurably better off by merging myself with their particular herd.

Growing Christmas trees is, by very definition, surely the very King of seasonal employments. You buy the seeds, you plant the seeds, you stand back from your handiwork, spade in hand, and – well, basically, you're done. That's what, eight hours tops?

What do you do for the rest of the year? Drive a cab? Run for Parliament? Write poetry? One envisages the members of the Christmas Tree Growers Association all congregating in an opium den in Limehouse for eleven months of the year, addled out of their brains with the fumes of soporific poppy, eking out the long empty days as they wait for their trees to grow by babbling nonsense to each other as they lie prostrate on their chaise-longues.

And who would join them? Why, all the other seasonal workers of course. Department Store Santas, Snow-plough drivers, professional tobogganists – all would be lying alongside them, stretched out in idle bliss (their boots left outside of course) happy in the knowledge that they don't have to lift a finger until the winter.

Time would drag. A certain listlessness would enter the conversation. Come summer and the talk would have strayed from Christmas trees to other things. By autumn they would be fed up with the sight of each other. Some would stumble about the opium den irritably, shouting "When will Christmas come? When, when, when!" –

before being led, sobbing, back to his chaise-longue by a patient attendant.

The Solstice would arrive. The trees have grown! For two weeks of the year the Federation of Christmas Tree Growers come into their own! They have a purpose in life! They pull on their Wellingtons with a bravado lacking in the previous months. They face the world with a smile, march confidently into their Christmas tree farms and face their fields proudly and happily. The four-by-fours arrive and beaming excited kids tumble out, running up and down the green rows of festive firs. The days pass in a blur of hacksaw and car-boot, chilly ankles and piped music. The last car pulls out of the yard. The dusk falls.

It is New Year. The Christmas Tree grower calls his Federation pals. And it's off to the opium den again. What a life.

Christmas Tree Grower Ken Hollingsworth of Bovingdon, Herts., wishing he'd listened to his Father and become a bathroom salesman.

English Society for Psychical Research

I'm becoming a little defensive during the course of writing this little book. As I set out, I was determined to dip my quill in acid and pen some withering satirical attacks upon the fools that form these absurd societies. But something has happened. Maybe I've mellowed with age, but in the three weeks I've been working on this volume, I have become increasingly protective of these groups. I've – I can hardly bring myself to say this – fallen in love with them.

I am no satirist. I'm not angry enough. I despise satire. I think it is the easiest of comic activities. Once Aristophanes had stood up and said the Athenian Government was corrupt, satire had said its piece. It was done. Of course satire should continue, and long may it do so – democracies need it. But it is, essentially, the same statement repeated over and over again, couched in a very slightly different joke. The statement is: people can be flawed, and corrupt. If I was a satirist and had to repeat this simple adage my whole life, I would be bored out of my mind. And what is more, if one gathered fifty satirists in a room, next door to fifty politicians, one would very probably find at least as many flawed and corrupt human beings amongst the satirists as one would amongst the politicians. I know some very dodgy satirists, with whom I certainly wouldn't trust my Grandmother.

So – the English Society for Psychical Research. Good luck to them, that's what I say. Are we psychic? Probably. I have some very strange hunches. Only this morning I kept getting images flashing in my mind of a bacon sandwich. And lo and behold, two hours later, I find myself having one for lunch. Spooky.

I am reliably informed by Wikipedia that the Society was formed by a group of eminent thinkers in 1882, and was the first organisation of its kind in the world, its stated purpose being "to approach these varied problems without prejudice or prepossession of any kind, and in the same spirit of exact and unimpassioned enquiry which has enabled Science to solve so many problems, once not less obscure nor less hotly debated."

A laudable mission-statement, and even more laudable modus operandi. This doesn't smack of a group of floridly-dressed women in long flowing scarves meeting clandestinely in various eccentric houses in Bayswater and, by candlelight, whispering and moaning to the ceiling to summon spirits of long-dead Hindus. This bespeaks an august, serious company, dedicated to a rational and scientific appraisal as to whether the hunches, flashes of inspiration (call them what we will), that we all of us experience from time to time, are evidence of a sub-conscious ability within the human organism to detect things prior to their proximate occurrence.

"There are more things in heaven and...." etc, and I will only proffer (as an amateur in these matters) my piecemeal knowledge that as instruments of observation we can perceive but a small fraction of the light spectrum: it is only after the invention of various - thingummies - that the infa-red and gamma spectri (?) became detectable. So if we cannot *see* everything around us - and that is a scientific fact - then why should it be absurd if we can 'feel' things without actually being able to spot them? With our eyes? In our heads? That's all I'm saying.

Members of the Society included luminaries from all walks of life from C.G. Jung to Alistair Sim. These are two men at the top of their respective professions. These are not lunatics. I... alright, enough. I feel like joining the Society for Psychical Research. They are clearly not the bunch of confidence tricksters that pop up in town halls in the North of England shouting "Is there a woman in the audience? A woman? I'm getting a woman please!" They are not of this ilk.

I could easily end this piece with a well-worn joke about trying to visit the Society but finding it closed owing to unforeseen circumstances. But I won't. I will end it by saying I don't *know* if the

Society for Psychical Research is correct. I just have a hunch they might be on to something.

Members of the Society for Psychical Research showing their trademark composure in the presence of a large ghostly arm.

The Pylon Appreciation Society

We've all seen pylons. They stalk our land like huge spidery-limbed creatures seemingly sprung from the teeming brain of Mr. H.G. Wells. They scar the skyline with stark jaggedness. Metal trees, they overshadow their more primitive benevolent wooden cousins in admonitory arrogant modernity. Where the friendly tree parades its form in random, chaotic thrusts and swoops of leaf and branch, the pylon strikes a malevolent, geometric pose.

You may conclude from the above somewhat florid paragraph that I myself do not appreciate pylons. But I do appreciate pylons. Whenever I boil an egg I appreciate pylons. But does my appreciation extend to the level of making day-trips to the blighters with a picnic hamper, and standing chatting about them with like-minded appreciators who, flasks in hand, swap anecdotes about their favourite specimens, even to the extent of producing notebooks and sketches of their discoveries? No.

An Italian fellow called Marinetti appreciated pylons - indeed, had he been alive today he would no doubt have been the "Pylon Appreciation Society's" Honorary President. Founder of the Futurist Movement in the Italy of the early twentieth century, Marinetti and his thrusting young Latin cohorts venerated all things modern: steam trains, viaducts, skyscrapers and, yes, pylons.

They are architecturally impressive, I'll give them that. Or should that be "Engineeringly" impressive? Their history has been chequered – many campaigned for cables to be laid underground, but as with the telegraph pole, the above-ground solution won the day, and our landscape was changed forever.

I have reached the thorny question of them being eye-sores. I wouldn't raise this at a meeting of the Pylon Appreciation Society. I'd be thrown out on my ear. But in the comfort of my own home I feel brave enough to raise it. So here it is: are pylons monstrous eye-sores and a blight upon our green and pleasant land?

I was fully prepared to disgorge venom at this point: give liberal vent to my spleen at the wanton destruction of the British countryside by these metallic denizens of the wire. And yet... when I thought about it more deeply, I came to the conclusion that the human eye and brain operates in a strange and opportunistic manner when confronted by changes in its environment. In short, it is surprising how easily pylons disappear from the mind when standing atop a pleasant hill and surveying a view. It's all a question of focus. If you think about pylons, you will see pylons. Mention the word pylon they will start springing up all around you like Orcs from the mud in 'Lord of the Rings.' But if you're on a walk and pylons are far from your mind, preoccupied as you are with such things, for example, as what you're going to have for dinner, or how to get your own back on that person who insulted you yesterday – as if by magic, not a pylon you will see. Even if you're actually surrounded by the wretched things.

This high-voltage pylon in Central Russia was recently pronounced 'The love of my life' by Ronald Corbett of Winnersh, Berkshire.

The mind will see what it wants to see. On a country walk we want to see fields, and woods, and birds, and sheep: so they are the things we see.

The metal giants stalking the plain melt phantom-like to the edges of our vision.

The founder of the Pylon Appreciation says on his website, *"It's funny how many people accuse me of being mad or geeky - and then they send me photos or ask for more information!"*

I'm not saying I'm a convert. Good heavens no. I don't *love* pylons. All I'm saying is that I took a photograph the other day of a pylon in the early morning mist. And I think it's pretty good. The pylon is stretching up into the morning sky and the mist is playing its wraith-like silks about its girders, and... well, I'm just wondering if they'd like to publish it on their website, that's all. Of course, I'd have to join the society, only as a means of getting my photographs on. Did I say one photo? Well, I meant ten.

The Exotic Animal Society

If you are at a loose end this weekend may I invite you to be envious of members of the Exotic Animal Society? They are, it seems, spoiled for choice. They could attend an 'Afternoon with a Reptile Vet' in Tiverton. Or they could pop along to the 'Portsmouth Ant Show.' Or, indeed, they could make a day of it and attend 'Llama Day' in Billericay.

I feel that my life is emptier for not owning an exotic pet. After returning from an afternoon's visit to the headquarters of the Exotic Animals Society I am beginning to cast resentful glances at my humble goldfish. I think he senses it too. I have one of their pamphlets: he can see what I'm reading through the glass of his bowl, and in the last few minutes he's definitely been making attempts to appear more exotic. He's just tried a back flip in order to impress me, and now he's dived behind a rock, probably to put on some flashy clothes.

According to the Exotic Animals Society I could fill the emptiness of my life very quickly by buying a Bearded Dragon or a Normal Female Corn

Snake. (What is an *Abnormal* Female Corn Snake? One that doesn't like corn? One that isn't even a snake?) Or I could impress my dog-walking friends by taking my Chilean Rose Tarantula for a stroll across the village green, or pop into the local café with my Giant Hissing Scorpion. Muzzled of course. I'm not sure the other patrons would like the hissing. Unless it coincided with the hissing of the espresso machine.

The owners of these exotic creatures possess, it is clear to me, a boredom threshold lower than the rest of us. Whereas we are content with rabbits and kittens, they must have wallabies and geckos. We pat our Jack Russells and put Iams out for our tabby's – they swim with their crocodiles or train their White Tree Frogs to jump through hoops. Show them a goldfish and they stifle a yawn; mention gerbils and they become comatose.

Yet I do not envy them. Especially when it comes to purchasing food for their pets. We pop a tin of Chum into our baskets, but they have to buy 'Lobster Roaches, ideal for Bearded Dragons, Water Dragons & other Reptiles: high shell to meat ratio, 20 adults for £2.00.' A bargain, I have no doubt, but I feel it would be a more pleasant experience to feed a small carrot to a bunny than chase Adult Lobster Roaches round the kitchen floor in order to stuff them, wriggling, into the gaping maw of a Commodo Dragon.

Or maybe not. Maybe I'm a boring soul.

The Institute of Nanotechnology

Nanotechnology has come a long way since the days when shrinking Racquel Welch to the size of a molecule and injecting her into the bloodstream of a scientist suffering from a blood-clot was a pretty cool achievement. To the Institute of Nano-technology today that's everyday stuff. Small beer. They're doing *really* small things now. Today it wouldn't be Racquel Welch, it would probably be Penelope Cruz, who's a lot shorter. And they wouldn't be injecting her into the bloodstream of a scientist. It'd be a mouse probably. Or an ant.

If I worked for the Institute of Nano-Technology, I'd forever be losing things. 'Ron, where did you put that subatomic mirochip?' 'It was on your desk the last time I saw it.' 'Well it's not there now. Have the cleaners been in?' It'd be a nightmare.

Just what is Nano-technology? Well, the Institute's website provides a clear mission statement: "Nanotechnology is an exciting area of scientific development that promises 'more for less.' It offers ways to create smaller, cheaper, lighter and faster devices that can do more and cleverer things." I am reliably informed that the materials members of the Institute work with are no bigger than a billionth of a metre, that is, the length of five hydrogen atoms. There are many advantages of this: chiefly, if you needed to take your work home, you wouldn't need a briefcase, you could carry it easily in a small pocket.

What are they making? Well, the Institute has its fingers in all sorts of pies – very small pies, obviously, like those snack pork pies you can get for parties. Fashion, electronics, the alternative energy industry, food – you name it, they can make it smaller. Waistcoats for termites, perhaps. Furniture for bees. The ultimate menu for obsessive dieters, including subatomic cakes and steaks no bigger than a quark. Nano Restaurants will spring up across the country where diners will be able to consume whole meals no bigger than a ladybird's eyebrow – and what's more, they won't have to use cutlery.

There is a natural air of suspicion surrounding all things Nano. My old Grandmother used to say 'What the eye don't see the heart don't grieve.' It was also the motto of a café I worked in as a youth – the 'Blue Danube' in High Wycombe, the kitchen of which at peak times resembled the mess hall during the Siege of Sebastopol. But would we embrace this proverb so carelessly if we knew the Nano-chaps had been messing with our grub? There's talk of governments authorising the insertion of all sorts of nano-vitamins, nanoadditives and what-nots into the nosh of the nation, in order to improve our overall health. Yet it would very difficult to prove that something a little shadier than a vitamin has been implanted into our pizza marguerite, given that the offending substance would be little bigger than a money-spider's wallet. There would only be one way to combat any abuse of the brave new nano-world we are entering: shrink Racquel Welch to the size of a pea and inject her into a pizza. I shall start working on the screenplay now.

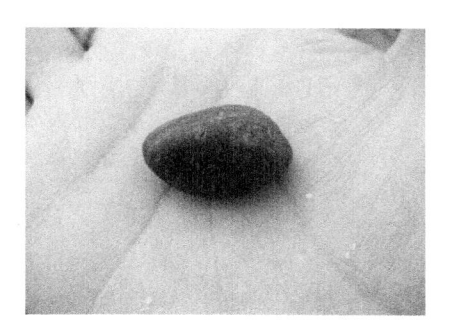

This is a small pebble. But it's not small enough to be of interest to any nano-technologist worth his salt.

The Ancient Order of Druids

The origin of this august society is shrouded in mystery, which is usually just a slightly exciting way of saying everyone's forgotten. The details we do have include that one Mr. Thurle founded it in a pub in Oxford Street, London, in 1781. He wasn't on his own. He had a few fellow merchants with him. I think most of the societies in this volume have been founded in pubs. I have founded several societies in pubs myself over the years. They have been somewhat short-lived, usually dissolving the next morning along with the alka seltzer tablets.

What is fascinating about the Ancient Order of Druids - and they're still in existence - is that they have nothing whatsoever to do with Druidism. In fact, they shun it completely, to the point where it is strictly forbidden to make any mention of either religion or politics in any of its numerous meeting halls. It's a bit like the Shropshire Scrabble League forbidding any games of scrabble on its premises, upon pain of dismissal. Or the Society for the Protection of Insects enshrining in its very constitution a statement that they are the sworn enemy of everything six-legged.

What is even more surprising is that the Society spread so quickly and successfully. Beginning in the Kings Head, Oxford Street, a second lodge was instituted at the Rose Tavern, Wapping, in 1783 – including no less a member than famed politician Charles Fox. What puzzles one is how on earth they publicised it, or went on a recruiting drive?

"We're thinking of starting a lodge here, the Ancient Order of Druids."

"Excellent – I'm sure there are quite a few locals very interested in old Celtic Religion; when's the first meeting?"

"No, no, um, I'd better say at this point that we're not actually Druids, and have no involvement in Celtic paganism."

"But you just said you're the Ancient Order of Druids."

"We are. But, er, we don't allow any discussion of Druidism."

"So why are you called the Ancient Order of Druids then?"

"I don't know. It just seemed like a good name."

"Hear that, Stanley – there's a bloke here who wants to start a lodge for the Ancient Order of Druids, but they're not actually Druids! You need to get your act together mate. What do you talk about then?"

"I don't know. Things."

"*Things?* You've started a society just to tall about 'things'? You don't need a Society to talk about things. I talk about things every day, and I don't belong to any Society."

"Look, can we start a lodge here or not?"

"How much will you pay for the weekly hire of the room?"

"Eight Shillings."

"No problem. See you next Wednesday."

Problems must have occurred when the *actual* Druids found out about their fake namesakes. They must have been outraged. "This is monstrous!" I believe was the actual phrase used by the Chief Druid. There were a flurry of court cases. "Chief Druid Barnstaple versus chief Druid Ramsbottom" is still spoken of in hushed whispers in Temple Inn.

And confusions must have been rife. Surely an *actual* Druid must have accidentally turned up to a meeting of the Ancient Order of (Non) Druids? - having seen, perhaps, a poster advertising the gathering? He'd arrive, all bright and bubbly, looking forward to a jolly evening's chinwag about all things Druidical. Imagine his disappointment when he found his Celtic conversation falling not only on deaf ears, but hostile ones.

"But I wanted to discuss the symbolic meaning of mistletoe!" he probably screamed as he was thrown out of the Rose Tavern, white robes flapping.

And today? I am told that the Ancient Order of Druids involve themselves in 'Social and Fraternal activities,' – that is, they meet in pubs and have the occasional raffle. They still don't talk about Druidism. You'd have thought that after over two hundred years of meeting in pubs and chatting they'd have run out of subjects to talk about that weren't Druidism. As time has worn on the topics would have been ticked off one by one, until one evening, as they sat twiddling their thumbs and idly sipping at their frothing pints, one member pipes up, hesitantly, "Um, I read this interesting book on old Celtic religion the other day."

He is met with cold hard stares.

"Shut it Colin. You know the rules."

"Yes, but we've run out of things to say! We've talked about everything else!"

"That's not true."

"Well what then? What haven't we talked about?"

"Lawnmowers. My neighbour's just bought a Baxter's 3-flywheel ZB."

"You mentioned that three weeks ago."

"Alright then. Figs."

"Figs?"

"Figs are interesting."

"No they're not."

"I find them fascinating."

"You're weird. I'm off to join the actual Druids."

"Traitorous bastard!"

Then someone remembered something that they hadn't talked about – marshmallows or something – everyone breathed a sigh of relief, Colin returned to his seat, and the Society lived to meet another day.

Mr. & Mrs Throgmorton - actual Druids, unlike the members of the Ancient Order of Druids.

The Prince Philip Movement

The most perplexing and somewhat worrying thing about this entry is that it describes itself as a *movement*. The word 'movement', smacking as it does of a growing political surge, indicates that its members appear to envisage a day when the Duke Edinburgh will become World President, or something similar.

Which in their eyes he is already. In fact, he is a God, which I think beats World President hands down. The Yaohnanen tribe on the southern island of Tanna in Vanuatu – I'm sure you've all been there – believe that the Duke of Edinburgh is the son of a Mountain Spirit who left his land to marry a powerful lady overseas. On two of those things they are, of course, correct.

The cult began in the 1950's and 60's when during a visit by the Royal couple the islanders witnessed the reverence and obsequy with which Queen Elizabeth was treated. They leapt to the obvious conclusion – and who wouldn't? – that her husband must be the brother of a Mountain Spirit. I mean it's obvious really.

Prince Philip knows of his divine status amongst the Polynesians and has paid several visits to the Yaohnanens. I bet he has. I mean, if you were worshipped as a god by the population of a remote island paradise, wouldn't you take every opportunity to pop over and soak up a bit of the old reverence? It would be churlish not to. I'd be nipping over there constantly. Frankly, if I was faced with either another wet weekend in Sandringham pottering about the library hands stuffed in pockets, followed by a desultory trip in the land-rover on yet another tour of the estate – or a couple of days under the Pacific sun, being feted by beautiful Polynesian maidens, being fed exotic fruit and generally leading the life of a Mountain Spirit, I know what I'd rather choose.

I do pity the Queen though. She's not worshipped – she is simply the "powerful lady" their god married. Over here, of course, she is the top dog, which is why Philip is probably cock-a-hoop when he gets the chance to pop over to Tanna. For most of the year he shuffles behind Her Majesty, at best getting a stinging headline in the papers about how he's offended some foreign dignitary or other: whereas over in Tanna he is the bee's knees, the top man, the Daddy. I bet he makes all sorts of excuses to his missus to go there as often as possible.

"Bye darling!"

"Where are you off to?"

"Me? Er - just popping out for a few partridge."

"But why have you packed a case?"

"I'm - having a picnic."

"Let me see that... you've packed tropical shorts!"

"It's pretty muggy out there."

"- and a short-sleeved floral shirt!"

"Give me that case back!"

"You're going to Tanna again aren't you?"

"Alright, yes, I'm going to Tanna - what of it? They like me in Tanna. I'm a god out there you know! I'll - see you in three days."

And three days later he returns with a tan and a smile on his face. He's had a weekend of being worshipped, and boy does it show.

As a Movement, the PPM presumably harbours ambitions for their cult to spread. They want Prince Philip to become the focus of an organised religion in the West to rival some of the top dogs, like Christianity or Scientology. I was going to express doubt over the soundness of such an aim, but since I've discovered that Jedi-ism is an officially recognised faith, I'm beginning to feel that one day, somewhere in England, there will be temples in various towns up and down the country which have as their altar-piece a magnificent image of our very own Duke of Edinburgh, rendered in Portland Stone and looking not only Royal, but veritably god-like.

The Nuwaubian Society

I am speechless on the subject of the Nuwaubian Society, so I will simply let their own manifesto of beliefs (judiciously edited to spare the feelings of the more tender-stomached among my readers) speak for them:

1. People were once perfectly symmetrical and ambidextrous, but then a meteorite struck the earth and tilted its axis causing handedness and shifting the heart off-centre in the chest.
2. Each of us has seven clones living in different parts of the world.
3. Women existed for many generations before they invented men through genetic manipulation.
4. Nikola Tesla came from the planet Venus.
5. Homo Sapiens are the result of cloning experiments that were done on Mars using Homo Erectus.
6. The Illuminati have nurtured a child, Satan's son, who was born on 6th June at the Dakota House on 72nd Street in New

York to Jacqueline Kennedy Onassis of the Rothschild/Kennedy families. The Pope was present at the birth and performed necromantic ceremonies. The child was raised by former US president Richard Nixon and now lives in Belgium, where it is now hooked up to a computer called "The Beast 3M," or "3666."

And these, I might add, are among the more sensible of their assertions. I won't even mention the one about snakes being the illegitimate children of George Bush, or how Rod Hull was assassinated by the Bilderberg Group for being the second cousin of Beelzebub.
b I do pity the Doctor who was brought in to deliver the son of Satan in New York. What if it was a junior Doctor's first job?

"Okay Ron, good news - you got your first delivery."

"Great!"

"It's a home birth - Dakota House on 72nd."

"Fantastic!"

"Yeah. So, good luck, and we'll see you later, and it's the Son of Satan. Now I'll be available if you need to - "

"Sorry?"

"What?"

"What did you just say? It's 'the son of Satan?'"

"Yeah."

"What are you talking about?"

"Look Ron, you wanted to be a midwife! You got to take the rough with the smooth."

"Rough with the smooth?! – you're asking me to deliver the offspring of the Devil?!"

"In a nutshell, yeah. But don't worry – the Pope will be there."

"The Pope?!"

"And Richard Nixon."

"Nixon? I'm outta here."

"Stay where you are! You've signed the Hippocratic oath haven't you? Nixon's there for a very good reason. He's going to adopt the kid and then send him to Belgium to hook him up to a computer."

"Have you been drinking?"

"Look, you've got to run. The clock's ticking – go go go!"

Apparently the Nuwaubians began as a perfectly legitimate – if somewhat extreme - Black Muslim group founded by one Dwight York in the early 60's, but when York was sent to jail the organisation started to drift. Mainly in the direction of complete and utter insanity.

I do not hope for much in this life. But I do hope for two things. One, I never want to meet a member of the Nawaubian Society. And two, I hope none of them ever become, or have ever been, a school-teacher.

Society for All Artists

I'm all for inclusiveness in clubs, but *all* artists? Please. For one thing, the logistics of the AGM would be a nightmare. Even the Albert Hall would be a squeeze. Some of them are quite slender like Tracy Emin but I've heard David Hockney has been getting a trifle paunchy lately so unless he keeps off the cheesecake it's got be the O2 or nothing.

I'd have stuck to genres if I were them. Society of Figurative Artists, Miniaturists, Abstract artists or whatnot. But *all* artists? A recipe for conflict if you ask me. I'd imagine that someone of the nature of Damien Hurst - broody, temperamental, avant-garde - would not easily share a dining table with the likes of Rolf Harris. I think there would be too many frosty silences, perhaps even culminating in a food fight.

Talking of food though, the main winner in this mad outburst of artistic inclusiveness must surely be the caterers. Picture the AGM. There'd be more finger-food than in those Iceland commercials. There'd be mountains of it. I'd like to be the company that supplied nibbles to 'all artists.' I'd boast about it for months. 'Who did you do last week Evelyn?' 'Ooh, some dull bank in the City. Lunch party. How about you?' 'All artists.' 'What, a party for some artists?' 'No, *all* artists.' 'All? No!' 'Yes. *All.*'

I'd put it on all my publicity material. Germany would be emptied of pigs simply to supply the sausage rolls alone. There'd be a cheesy wotsit shortage. Governments would debate long and hard into the night on the scarcity of the hula-hoop.

And what would they talk about at their AGM's, all these artists? They'd all want to bang on about their own stuff of course. Fights would break out. 'Installations are better than portraits!' someone would cry, and paint-stained fists would be raised. It'd be a bit like gathering every single actor in the world in a big tent and expecting the conversation to range beyond their next job or how their agent is holding them back.

I don't want to veer off into a debate on modern art, but one point must be made. There are far more artists around nowadays, aren't there? I mean, in decades gone by one would have to be pretty good in order to describe oneself as an artist at social gatherings and such like. Now, however, one can simply put a packet of sausages on a shoebox and bob's your uncle you've got 'artist' on your passport. Who started it? Well, Andy Warhol I guess. As soon as he said a soup-can is art, the floodgates were opened to mediocrity. That's not to say Warhol was mediocre – he was a pioneer who at least had some draughtsmanship. Others came along who said slabs of paint were art – and they are: I am gazing at a Roethke as I write and am entranced by the natural tones, abstract though they are. But when the art schools start telling their students that if they dress up as Shirley Temple and stuff a duffle bag full of cheesy wotsits, and that if they then stand in a corner of the Tate they have an objective entitlement to be judged alongside J.M.W. Turner – well, that's when my appreciation of the New starts to waver.

They're happy of course. For the mildly talented it was a wonderful day when the art establishment pronounced anyone could be an artist. A similar thing happened to the world of television. When I was young one could turn on the TV and be pretty confident one would be able to spend an evening looking at a range of people pretty talented in their own way: an interviewer, mayhap, or an actor, singer, dancer, comedian. Now one switches on the TV and one spends an evening watching a model talk about her bulimia, and a wealthy couple from Chiswick look for a place in the South of France, while keeping a crash-pad in the capital, and a wealthy air-head from SW3 gossip about her girlfriends behind their backs.

Democracy has wielded its garden roller and delivered its message: all culture shall be flattened into one amorphous shape. We're all the same. I'm an artist, you're an artist, I'm a TV star, and you're a TV star.

So I shall be attending the next meeting of the Society of All Artists. I'm entitled to. Have I exhibited? Ugh, the very thought. I do not 'make works.' I'm a Situationist. I travel round the London tube system and, stopping at every tenth station, hand out a packet of liquorice all-sorts to the first vicar I see. That is my art. You see, I'm no good at drawing and painting, and I'm lazy. I've got a lot of time on my hands. But it's alright. Charles Saatchi and the ICA say that's okay.

Companions of the Crow

Of the numerous Battle Re-enactment Societies I could have included in this volume I have settled upon the Companions of the Crow. Why? I'll tell you in a minute. Hang on.

As I say, there are hundreds I could have picked. I think I remember someone telling me once that all of us, at any one time, are no more than ten feet away from a re-enactment society. Or is that rats? Every single conflict is catered for, from the Campaigns of Genghis Khan to the War of Captain Jenkins' Ear. They range from societies devoted to reliving comparatively civilised engagements such as the 'Battle of Henley Fort' to frankly uninhibited and somewhat rapacious clubs like 'The Dogs of War.'

I do not think I would like to belong to 'The Dogs of War.' The name alone suggests that its members harbour motives that extend beyond the desire to learn from simple historical dramatic reconstruction. To be blunt, they sound as if they want to actually kill people. If I was a parish councillor in charge of a village green and got a call from 'The Dogs of War' asking if they could use our local greensward for their afternoon of shenanigans, I would at the very least politely suggest it be put to the Entertainments committee for rubber-stamping.

For most re-enactment societies, however, historical exactitude rather than the love of a good punch-up is the prime motor of their activities. The Sealed Knot, for example - perhaps the most noteworthy of these organisations - are a force for good in the realm of education: their costumes precise, their weapons exact, their reconstructions perfect. Stumble across one of their gatherings whilst on a country ramble and one would leap to the understandable conclusion that one had travelled back in time. I have observed these chaps (& wenches) put on their displays at local museums and such, and I returned from the experience with ears still ringing from the musket-blasts and a sense of admiration for their accuracy.

Other re-enactment societies are not so pernickety, and say so openly in their mission statements. Which brings me to 'The Companions of the Crow.' First, the very name suggests those video games you see advertised (are they still called video games? - I'm not so sure. I remember when they were called 'Etching Games) – that dwell in a fantastical realm of 'Olden Days' or 'Days of Yore' – a vague universe of castles, massive knights and busty maidens. Such a world I imagine the Companions of the Crow to inhabit. Who was this Crow anyhow? I studied history pretty deeply when I was a bespectacled nipper and I don't recall anyone called Crow, notable or otherwise. And I certainly don't recall if he had any friends

Secondly, and more importantly, their constitution states: 'While we try to be as authentic as possible in everything we do, we are not able to say 'this is how it was,' only 'this is a close approximation to how we think it might have been.' A dictum so wonderfully vague that surely it gives members carte blanche to do almost anything. Take a kalashnikov along? A bazooka? A scene springs to mind of a group of chain mail clad chums of the popular Crow bracing themselves for an attack by fellow 'enemies' of the said winged creature, and seeing a Chieftan tank roll advancing towards them. "Whoah!" one of them utters, lowering his lance. "Just hold on a second now. Is that Kevin?"

It is. The same Kevin shoves the brakes of the tank on and it grinds to a halt in the Sussex meadow. Silence falls. The birds sing. The lid of the turret opens. Out pops Kevin's head.

"Problem?"

The medievally-clad buddies of the Crow gather round the metal monster that has appeared amongst them like a green vision.

"You've gone too far this time Kevin," "I thought we were a medieval re-enactment society?" – while some of the younger pals of the raven let their youth get the better of them and begin cooing over the machine: "Wow, it's great isn't it?" "Where'd you get it?"

Kevin's defence is that there is nothing in the Society's constitution that forbids the utilisation of advanced heavy weaponry. The said constitution is fetched. The members spend an hour poring over it. Tea is drunk.

"There," says Kevin, jabbing at a sentence on page eight. "A close approximation to what we think it might have been!"

"A close approximation? It's a tank!"

The argument rages long into the afternoon, until someone lugs over a crate of Kingfisher cider and the talk strays from historical accuracy to the subject of the football match the following day.

Companions of the Crow are, then, not so much an historical re-enactment society, as an *imaginative* re-enactment society. And all the better they are for it.

The Small Coal-man's Club

In all the dusty annals of recorded 'clubbism' perhaps none are more redolent of associative eccentricity than the above-titled.

The eighteenth century was, indisputably, the Golden Age of clubs. London was brimming with them. Gather a few gentlemen in an ale-house, ignite a conversation with a chance remark tossed like a spark into a pile of tinder – and bob's your uncle, a club is born. Some were noble, with mission-statements far-reaching and of national – nay, planetary – influence. Of these must be included the Royal Society, founded in the last years of the seventeenth century and numbering among its members such luminaries as Wren & Newton; the Athenaeum, that august collection of literary and artistic worthies; and indeed the Whigs themselves, who metamorphosed of course into the Liberal party.

Others were not so august. Indeed, they smacked of the appellation 'July.' They had humbler aims, narrower remits. Such was the Small Coal-man's Club. Little is known of this association, apart from the fact that it was probably founded by a deliverer of coal whose stature could not, and would never be, described as gargantuan. That much we can settle upon as bearing the epithet 'true.' Quite why this diminutive deliverer of fuel decided one day to bind himself, by something stronger than mere friendship, to another of his ilk – to whit, a dwarfish purveyor of carbon-based energy – is lost in the cobwebs of antiquarian speculation. Various theories have been propounded: a London-wide conspiracy of coalmen of the larger sort against their less bulkier cousins? – inspiring a sense of collectivism amongst the latter in order to defend their interests? Perhaps. Some less imaginative theorists have asserted that it wasn't the Coalmen at all who were small, but the coal itself – i.e. the association was formed as a kind of union the purpose of which was simply to carry diminutive portions of the black stuff to the citizens of London – who maybe had small grates. Or perhaps the Coalmen had small hands. Both ideas have been rejected by every sensible person as being preposterous. Quite frankly I don't know why I even mentioned them. Sorry.

Another slightly more convincing notion has been entertained by – well, by me, chiefly. To outwit their muscular and more lumbering colleagues, who were able by mere dint of their proportions to deliver larger quantities of the essential warmth-giving crumbly stuff to the customers, swathes of little coalmen hit upon a plan whereby, if they could not deliver *as much* as the big coalmen, they could nevertheless deliver their loads more *quickly*. That is to say, down the chimney. Were the rooftops of London town crowded with tiny proletarians who, like so many sooty little Santas, scampered across the pan-tiles and tipped their goods down the chimneypots of their paying clients, thus beating their tall rivals who were still heaving their massive sacks from their carts in the middle of the road down below?

I plump for the latter. It would make for a few dusty parlours, but what the heck.

Randolph Nutmeg, at 4ft 8 inches a shoe-in as 13th President of the Small Coal-man's Club.

The Society for Creative Anachronism

Have we evolved into a desk-bound species of computer-gazers whose muscular and spiritual decline is proceeding in direct proportion to our addiction to the idiots lantern of the pc? The Society for Creative Anachronism think so. They are the new Luddites of our brave new world. They would have us smash our computers and dance off across the meadows to our workshops, and start weaving or something. I'm all for that. I like dancing. I don't like weaving though. My creative anachronism might stop at the odd display of medieval Terpsichore. Don't get me to weave. Please.

The Society for Creative Anachronism is tapping into what I feel is a perennial trait in human nature: that of a nagging discontent with ones present. We've all felt it. We all hanker for the days when our home town didn't have all these bloody roundabouts and bypasses and superstores and I remember when it was all fields round here! But if you think this is a malaise peculiar to our times, then think again. Thomas Hardy chronicled the pining of the agricultural communities of the 1890's for the pre-technological age. And even in 1590 they were not immune to nostalgia: the antiquarian John Stow in his mighty 'Survey of London' spent many paragraphs complaining of the destruction of the particular metropolitan neighbourhood he had known as a child – and that was before Tescos.

So it's not just us who are at some level deeply troubled by progress and who feel the pang for what we imagine to be a more spiritually nourishing and pleasant time. Only our expression of it seems that much more pervasive than our predecessors. Proof of the pervasiveness of our contemporary hunger for the past we have come up with a whole genre of television programmes, a genre which might have been created by the SFCA itself: 'Edwardian Farm,' 'Victorian Chemist', '1950's School.' Life is slipping by so fast and the pace of its visible changes so swift that we feel ourselves clinging on to the old ways with mental whitened knuckles. We are hypnotised by antiques: we pore over them like elephants browse through the bones of their ancestors: it is our way of giving silent worship to our long-dead predecessors.

Our love of the past, as I say is not peculiar to us: and therefore has a deeper source. My personal theory is this: our desire to recreate the manners, dress and technology of a prior age is one method of draining ourselves of – in Richard Dawkin's phrase – the 'anaesthetic of familiarity.' Dressing up in Tudor clothes in a field outside Faversham, and spending an afternoon weaving a rush mat, is Clive Simmons' way of forgetting for a brief afternoon that he is a marketing executive who works for 'Exo-Plaz Digital Turbo-Flex Ltd.' in Sunbury.

So long live the Society for Creative Anachronism. There are many days when I feel anaesthetised by too much familiarity. Some take drugs – I would prefer to pop along to a meeting of the SFCA and wear a doublet for a couple of hours. And maybe eat some pottage. I don't know what pottage is - which is, of course, the reason I would eat it.

The Split-Farthing Club

If you were passing the Old Queen's head in Bishopsgate in the year 1765 and chanced to pop in for a noggin - presuming, of course, you were out of noggins - you may very well have spotted a group of decidedly miserable looking fellows huddled in the snug bar raising a glass of water to their cracked, parched lips.

You would be in the presence of the members of the notorious 'Split-Farthing Club.' This was a club of misers.

When I was a boy the word 'miser' had a powerful authority. Everyone knew a miser. There was a miser in everyone's home town. It verged on the legally obligatory. It was almost a job, like coalman, or sweetshop-owner.

A miser could be either male or female, and usually shuffled around the locality in a greasy coat. It helped matters if they were slightly bent over and occasionally laughed softly to themselves. You'd hear the adults mention them, and then that word would crop up: *miser*. "So-and-so's a miser," they'd murmur, and everyone would nod. "All alone in that big house. Must be worth a fortune." And then misers would crop up in books, of course, their patron saint being, naturally, Ebenezer Scrooge.

In the small town where I grew up there lived a man whom we simply called 'William.' He inhabited a rickety wooden house with a veranda at the top of our lane, and lived with his mother. To us he was elderly, so she must have been ancient. Ragged lengths of dirty cloth that perhaps once were curtains hung in the windows in shabby sun-faded strips. The house was surrounded by a tangled thatch of overgrown bushes and weeds and some of the panes of glass were cracked or broken. Inside it was not much different, except that it was overgrown with rubbish – old newspapers littering the floor, bags of stuff sitting fat and obscure in various corners.

As William got older and more infirm us local boys used to run errands for him. It was in the days when shops would give you money for returning their bottles. And William had many. Ginger beer, lemonade, Tizer. He'd give us as many as we could carry and we'd struggle down the steep lane to the shop and then back up the hill to give him his earnings – receiving, for our trouble, the sum of two-pence per trip.

As a child I had other things on my mind than discovering more about this strange figure who, like a fairytale character, dwelt amongst us but seemed not of this world. He was just a colourful local we enjoyed doing errands for because doing so was like walking into a story. Today of course, these characters, these 'Misers', would be diagnosed with obsessive-compulsive disorder and probably offered some kind of therapy.

The members of the Split-Farthing Club were clearly of that shade of unhingement. But of course in the eighteenth century, mental illness was very simplistically defined: if you ranted and raved and foamed at the mouth, you were mad. If you didn't rant and rave and foam at the mouth, you were not mad. It must have been very easy being a psychiatrist in those days. If you just hoarded stuff and wandered around slightly bent over in a greasy coat, you weren't mad at all, you were simply a Miser, which was fine.

Hence the semi-respectability of the Split-Farthing Society. They clearly suffered from behavioural problems akin to the above-described, but instead of being shunned and mocked, the Society became well-known as a resource for coming up with ways of saving money. People would seek their advice. Their tips were sometimes published – a bit like during the Second World War when advice on scrimping and saving was dispensed in column inches in various household magazines or in stilted Government films.

The fact that the members of the Split-Farthing Club bonded together in the first place seems evidence, to me, that their mental eccentricities were not debilitating. They clearly wanted to put their prudence to practical use. It was a bit like sufferers of vertigo forming a trade union, pooling their knowledge on the best ways to avoid high places.

Members of the Club became famous, for their appellations if not for their parsimony: Sir John Pick-Plumb, and the fantastically-named Buggeranto Covert, who 'died in his own dung'. Sadly, there are no records of the content of the meetings. Methods of increasing stinginess no doubt abounded.

A friend recently suggested that the current world recession might very well usher in a new era of 'make do and mend.'

He might be right. In which case, I feel it would be highly appropriate to proceed at once to the Old Queen's Head in Bishopsgate, and resurrect the Split-Farthing Club. I will contact George Osborne at once. He could be its Honorary President.

The Ejection Tie Club

The above-named corp. was founded in 1958 by Sir James Martin CB MA Bai CENG FIMecE FRAeS. I haven't made those letters up. They all mean something very very good.

If, one weekend, you find yourself meandering along the winding lanes and across the fragrant buttercup meadows around Denham, South Buckinghamshire, then the chances are that after a time you will hear a certain noise, and stop in your tracks.

That noise is a not-unpleasant distant drone, akin to that of a lazy insect. It will seem far away, like all sounds in summertime seem. But it will get louder, and then you will see a single-engined plane suddenly swoop into view, perhaps encircling the field before descending to a hidden runway beyond the hedgerow.

For this part of England abounds with airfields. And with airfields come aeronautical engineering companies - for aeroplanes have to be tinkered with, fixed, patched up. Such a company is Martin Baker Associates. They have been working out of Denham for more than sixty years, and they are famous for two things: inventing and designing the best ejection seats in the world: and founding the glorious Ejection Tie Club.

There are many clubs in this book which one might not perhaps hanker to be a member of. The Ejection Tie Cub might well feature high on that list. For to qualify as a member you have to have undergone nothing less than successfully ejecting from a crashing plane. I say successfully. That is obvious really. I do not think that the Ejection Tie Club would like to seek you out as a member if your ejection had not resulted in you retaining your rude health.

Since its foundation the club has welcomed more than a hundred ejectees into its aeronautical bosom, from all across the world – for the Martin Baker Ejector seat has been sold to more than 55 air round the globe. If a pilot runs into trouble, and is forced to leave the aircraft, preferably at great speed, then there are two comforting thoughts that he can treasure as he whistles through the vacant air earthward. One: the Martin Baker Ejector Seat seems to have worked, and two: I will shortly be welcomed into the glorious ranks of the Ejection Tie Club.

Such is the privilege of being a member that the rules of entry are, of necessity, strict as a governess. For members are afforded that wonderful prize that extends way beyond the ownership of a tie, silk-embroidered or otherwise. For members have the lifelong privilege of having a life-saving anecdote to tell. In bars, at dinner-parties, wherever there hovers a receptive ear. Non-members are easily distinguished from members. The former huddle in a silent group at the Aerodrome bar, sipping their gin and tonics in a desultory manner and gazing sulkily at a livelier crowd at the other end. This latter group are animated, transfixed. For a Member is telling his or her story.

And what a story it is. We have no need to go into details here, suffice to say the retelling of it involves a lot of hand gestures, where the arms become wings, and the miming abilities of the anecdotalist are tested like never before. At the apex of the story the tellers' arms shoot up into the air to signify the opening of the chute and their clutching thereof; their lower body then assumes a kind of sitting position to indicate the comfort of the Martin-Baker seat – 'it's upholstered, you know!' They sway gently in the breeze if the day of their escape was calm; they rock violently from side to side if it was not. Their story comes to a close and the listeners, to a man, burst out in a spontaneous ripple of applause. At the other end of the bar the non-members gaze on, taking sulkiness and envy to new levels. Then someone hands round the peanuts and they start discussing Sunday League football.

Such is the kudos of membership of this organisation that it has, over the years, attracted no small measure of attempted deceit. The most famous case was that of Norman Coolidge, a weekend daylight pilot. Mr. Coolidge's favourite films were 'Reach for the Sky,' and 'Battle of Britain.' Enough said. Mr. Coolidge's desire to impress young ladies resulted in him trying, no less than eleven times, to gain a coveted tie by leaving his aircraft at high speed. Yet to this day he has not been awarded one. Why? Well, for the simple fact that on each occasion of departure from his vehicle, he has – there's no other way to put this – either been on the ground during ejection, or there has been absolutely nothing wrong with his plane.

Such was Coolidge's initial fear of ejecting whilst airborne, that he decided that by far the best way of obtaining the sought-after neckerchief, would be simply to find a lonely spot somewhere, land his single-engined Cessna, press the ejector button, and bob's your Uncle. He would then drag the seat a few hundred yards away, and await rescue.

The Airfield authorities were having none of it. Questions were asked – chiefly, how on earth did the plane land itself after Coolidge's departure from it? The obtuse Coolidge stared at them blankly, and offered up no answer. He hadn't thought it through.

Steeling himself, Coolidge realised that in his subsequent attempts an ejection whilst actually airborne must feature prominently in the escapade. And so it was that he began his monthly ejections. Club members would be gathered in the Airfield Bar chatting over drinks, there'd be a buzz from a Cessna flying overhead, the engine would suddenly cut out, followed by the sharp noise of a small explosion, the members would look at each other and nod, and mutter – 'Coolidge' – and sure enough, five minutes later there would be a muffled thud of an ejector seat landing on the airfield, followed by a more distant explosion of crashed Cessna.

All in all Coolidge got through ten planes. It cost him a fortune. He was never awarded a tie – the Club saw through all his attempts. Just as the Labour politician Denis Healy is described by commentators to the 'best Prime Minister we never had,' so Norman Coolidge is spoken of as the 'Best ejector the Ejection Tie Club never had.'

The Association of Dead People

Call me fussy but I can think of several better ways of spending my evenings than sitting in a village hall surrounded by cadavers. Accuse me of rampant selfishness if you will but even the prospect of a night spent playing cribbage would gladden my heart more than sitting slumped in a circle trying to extract conversation from a collection of corpses. Even rafia-weaving might hold more appeal to me. But that's just me. It's just the way I am.

Of course I jest. I wouldn't even be let in to the Association of Dead People. For a start, my smile and attempt to shake the chairman's hand would be a blatant giveaway that perhaps I wasn't fully qualified for membership. And of course, the chairman would be dead anyway so would be unable to shake my hand. Both of us would be frozen in a kind of perplexed stand-off – the perplexity being largely my own.

There is one advantage to the Association of Dead People, and that is the complete lack of dispute amongst its members. As a result of a complete absence of breath, and indeed, all bodily functioning, there would doubtlessly be a consequent refreshing lack of argument and controversy amongst its members.

In one huge sense of course each one of us will become a member of the Association of the Dead. And I feel that after such a profound thought I need to pause for a cup of tea and a melancholy stare out of the window.

The Association of Dead People, of course, is not a society comprising stiffs. It has a serious, moral and political purpose. It stems from a heinous practice in India, particularly Uttar Pradesh, of falsely declaring someone dead by means of bribing officials, and then seizing – perfectly legally – the land belonging to the supposedly departed citizen.

Such a citizen was Lal Bihari, who founded the Association in the 1980's and was in fact "dead" from 1976 to 1994. He even used the word *Mritak* (Dead) in his name during the period.

I can only imagine what it must be like to walk around and try and lead a perfectly normal life when all the time other people think you are dead. It would certainly put the wind up your colleagues at work. I'd go in dressed in a sheet just to add a little frisson to the occasion. And as for trying to hold a conversation, let alone have an argument – well, you'd be on a hiding to nothing. 'You're dead!' your arguee would proclaim, 'you have no opinion! In fact, I can't even hear you!' Then they'd put their fingers in their ears and go 'la la la' like a six year old.

'If life serves you lemons, then make lemonade,' they say. If I became a member of the Association of Dead People I'd try and make a go of it. For a start, I'd dress up as a ghost (see above). I'd also walk into shops and stuff my pockets with free food. After all, they can't prosecute a dead person! You could do anything. They couldn't touch you.

I feel that the members of the Association of Dead People are thinking of themselves too much as victims. They're not focussing on the advantages that quite clearly accrue when the world thinks you're a gonner. For as Shakespeare might have put it, 'When we have shuffled off this mortal coil, we can very easily pop into Londis and take a pork pie without fear of the consequences.'

The League of Moveable Type

I am immediately suspicious of any society which begins its publicity material with the words *"No more bullshit."*

I could understand if the organisation was a political one whose members had been forced to band together as a consequence of being lied to consistently over a period of years – by ones nations' leaders perhaps, or unscrupulous, ruthless bosses, leading to an outcry of 'enough!' But this is not the case. Read more of their introductory material and it slowly dawns on one that the League of Moveable Type is an association dedicated to the development of new fonts.

Now, like you, I have my favourite fonts. In my working life I mainly use the same one. Perhaps two. I feel – and this is just my gut talking – that we have enough fonts. But no. The League of Movable type asserts – in a manifesto no less, like the nascent communist party or Prince Kropotkin's anarchists – that these fonts are nothing more than "bullshit."

I have no strong feelings either for against any font. I do not discriminate. But these chaps clearly do. their hatred of certain fonts has plainly reached boiling point. I feel sorry for them. Are there not worthier causes in the world meriting the cry "No more bullshit!" than computer typefaces? TV advertising for one, or celebrity magazines. I would rather shout "No more bullshit!" to a copy of "Closer" magazine than Baskerville Old Face, quite frankly.

I applaud the aims of the League of Movable Type. I would not ban them from coming up with new fonts. There are worse ways humans can spend their day than sitting round coming up with new ways of shaping their letters. I would not ban anyone from doing anything harmless to others.

Yet I have a caveat. Do we actually *need* any more fonts? It's a bit like fruit. Do we need any more types of fruit? I wouldn't ban a horticulturalist from crossing a tangerine with a kumquat, but I wouldn't urge him to do it as a matter of necessity. I would tolerate the experiment, then gently suggest he move on to more pressing matters. Ditto fonts. Surely they are the toys of writers, not their tools. For those who praise style over substance, but all means, focus on the font over the content. Just don't get me involved. I'm content with the courier, thanks. It was good enough for the faded millions of typewriters of generations past, so it is good enough for me.

I think the cry of "No more bullshit" is perhaps directed not so much at the finite number of fonts provided by Microsoft Word, but probably at the company itself. It is born from a childish resentment that we should be dictated to in the first place: who are you to tell me what fonts I can use? I'll invent my own fonts thank you! And they stomp off and form the League of Moveable Type.

I've seen a few of the fonts invented by the League. They are fine. They are inventive. They are, in short, fonts. Good luck to them. I write for a living and I've only ever used three fonts at most. Yet there are a lot of things in society that we have a lot of. So why not, I say. Let's have a lot of fonts. It's the League bit I'm a little wary of. And the passion. Yeats said "The worst are full of passionate intensity," and I'm pretty sure he wrote that line after met a font designer in Dublin who had suggested to him over a Guinness that they ransack print shops across the city demanding "No more bullshit."

The Milton Keynes Ghost Club

The number of societies devoted to lusting after the spectral - that is to say, seeking out evidence of the after-life - runs into the thousands. I was therefore spoilt for choice as to who to investigate. There are Ghost Clubs in Canada, Fiji, and Stockport. Their members range from Professors of Economics to tea-ladies for obscure public relations firms on the Devon-Cornish border. They organise weekly ghost-watches, spend nights out in various sinister old houses and castles (tickets very reasonably priced) and - if they're lucky to have a friend who knows someone who knows a Channel 5 producer - they might get to appear on one of the many 'ghost-watch' programmes currently ubiquitous in our television schedules.

There is the Hounslow Ghost Club, the Billericay Phantom Society, the Afterlife League of Mid-Glossop. A little further West you will find the Spectre-Finders of Outer Kettering, the South Rutland Association of Ghoul-Spotters, and the Peebles Poltergeist Patrol. There is even '*The* Ghost Club,' - which clearly considers itself so far superior to the others it has abandoned a place-name in favour of the definite article.

The latter was formed at Cambridge University and boasts hundreds of famous past members from Charles Dickens to Peter Cushing. In 2012 it is celebrating its 150th anniversary, and is publishing a chronicle of its illustrious fright-coveting history.

I chose to visit the Milton Keynes Ghost Society. They have not published a chronicle of their history. They're hardly old enough to even have a history. Which is why, perhaps, I chose to visit them and not another, more heritage-soaked organisation. As a gleaming New Town, I thought, a child of the 60's, how old can its ghosts be? Surely the most ancient ghoul stalking its broad boulevards and sparkling shopping malls could only be some unfortunate town-planner who fell down a manhole in 1967?

There are no sinister castles or spooky old manor houses in the environs of Milton Keynes. (Or so I thought – see below). Would any self-respecting ghost, I wondered, be seen dead on Midsummer Boulevard, or plying its ghastly trade along the cycle lanes of Secklow Gate? Do headless horsemen, when offered the chance to gallop through either the winding lanes of medieval Canterbury, or past DFS Furniture in Silbury Retail Park, MK, choose the latter without the slightest evidence of hesitation?

My scepticism was soon to be roundly demolished. For imagine my amazement when I learned that Milton Keynes hadn't sprung from the brain of a 60's town planners' committee at all, but was derived from an ancient village of the same name. Are you imagining my amazement? Good. Milton Keynes village is still in existence and lurks somewhere, hidden from the public gaze, away from the retail parks and the cycle lanes and the roundabouts. I paid it a visit, and it consists of little more than a collection of rural cottages and a thatched pub. But as a setting for ghostly sightings, it's up there with Hampton Court.

Roger Mullet's drawing of the menacing apparition he saw outside the shopping centre, Milton Keynes, on the evening of July 10th, 2019.

So good luck to the Milton Keynes Ghost Club. Next time you pop up to the Bowl to see JLS, do not drive home immediately afterwards. Seek out the mysterious ancient village in its midst. Linger awhile at its pump. Wander past the old inn and up the dusty lane by the churchyard, and pause awhile. Stare at the moon caught in the tangled branches of a tree.

What was that noise? An owl? - or the plaintive cry of a long-dead washerwomen executed in 1701 for murdering eight minstrels?

Probably an owl.

The Man-Hunter's Club

The contemporary teenager is a much-maligned member of our society. But is our century unique in possessing in our midst a race of nascent adults whom we have grown, quite frankly, to fear? Were our ancestors similarly beset by hordes of cynical, borderline criminal sections of society whose devil-may-care weltanschaung spills over on too many occasions into destructive hatred of order and safety?

The answer is yes, judging from an hours' perusal of the annals of the eighteenth century Man-Hunter's Club.

Born, once again, in the Golden Age of Clubbism, (the oft-unaptly termed Age of Reason, the eighteenth century), the notorious Man-Hunter's Club comprised a group of raggedly organised folk in their pre-adult years -18-odd - who were wont to gather in the ale-houses and inns of old London Town for a night's carousing.

After drinking their fill, they would then spill out onto the cobbled streets, and staggering and stumbling, would make their way to a pre-selected square or park. Usually they favoured the Inns of

Court, those vast areas of old London that often lurk behind the facades of the main thoroughfares like Holborn, Chancery Lane and the Strand, and which consist of ancient warrens of buildings and staircases arranged around a spacious common of lawn, trees and benches. Here the lawyers reside, those armies of wigged and gowned pillars of our world-renowned British judiciary.

The members of the Man-Hunter's Club would then find a suitable bush or tree, or clump of shrubs, and lurk there, stifling giggles, and lie in wait for their first victim.

The Man-Hunter's Club were not particularly fussy, but their choice of victim was not wholly random. An ideal candidate would be a middle-aged man of - to them - humorous appearance, that is to say, his gait and manner would signal to them a certain ripeness for jocularity in pursuit. The best examples were the dignified: barristers, curates and the like, or haughty clerks perambulating with noses in the air.

They would then give chase.

What first sprang into the minds of the chasees only conjecture can supply. To witness a gaggle of youths spring from behind a shrub in an advanced state of inebriation, shrieking and bellowing, arms flailing, must have inspired in the heart and mind of the innocent victim a terror so instant that it might have been borne from a vision of hell itself. Legal books must surely have been tossed into the air in fright, and lungs must have been exerted to bursting point as the legs pumped up and down in a desperate effort to propel oneself across the empty space between capture and safety.

The safety was usually an inn. An inn has a crowd, and there is safety in numbers. Once there, the fugitive would sink to his knees on the floor of the public bar and – gasping and pointing a quivering finger in the direction of his now-absent hunters – be revived by a shot or two of rum.

I say 'now-absent hunters' because – and this was a Cardinal Rule of the Man-Hunter's Club – the participants were sworn never to actually catch up with any of their quarries. The raison-d'etre of the Club was simple pursuit, and nothing else. To catch would be to lose. As soon as the hunted reached civilization, the hunters would fade into the darkness, not to be seen for another week until they chose to resume their athletic activities.

I am ambivalent towards the Man-Hunter's Club. The image of an elderly lawyer's clerk legging it across a moonlit park being pursued by young laughing tearaways is, one has to admit, highly Pickwickian.

Yet if it was us who was being chased, their air would be blue with curses and promises of revenge. Our attitude towards young scallywags has always had this inconsistency. We envy their sense of fun, and if we are in a good mood we chuckle at their antics. But if we are on the receiving end of their shenanigans then we become middle-aged curmudgeons and rail against the moral turpitude of the generation that will replace us.

My jury is out on the Man-hunters Club.

The Beggar's Club

I was at first loath to include this club in the book. Begging is a poignant activity at the best of times. If beggars want to formalise their bond and set up a society, a union, good luck to them.

But on closer examination of the Beggar's Club (as with several other clubs in this book I am indebted to that wonderful archivist of odd associations Edward Ward, whose 'Compleat & Humorous Account of all the Remarkable Clubs & Societies in the Cities of London & Westminster' of 1745 contains a wealth of invaluable material for the connoisseur of the Odd) it becomes clear that the Beggar's Club of that era was nought but a conglomeration of the counterfeit. To wit, a union of *fake* beggars.

Bogus beggary is a long-standing profession in England. Shakespeare alluded to it. For the first ten years of his career as a playwright in London the Bard lived in Bishopsgate, opposite Bethlehem Hospital – Bedlam. Founded in 1247, the asylum would have been very familiar to Shakespeare as he would have passed it as he walked to and fro on his way to work at either the

Curtain or the Theatre in Shoreditch. Fake insanity was a popular ploy amongst itinerants, and surely we have a fine example of Shakespeare writing from life when we see Edgar in King Lear metamorphose into poor *Tom o'Bedlam* - the nickname for the perpetrators of false madness, possessed as he was with the spirits of Mohad and Flibertigibbet. Was the playwright remembering the numerous imitation lunatics he must have stepped over on the pavement during his daily journey to and from work throughout the 1590's? And the feigned madness of Hamlet - was that fleshed out with snatches of overheard garbled monologue from the counterfeit lunatics who paraded Bishopsgate Street from dawn to dusk?

These counterfeit crackpots were the first members of what became a large and august society, albeit an underground one - for begging of any kind was illegal, let alone fraudulent roadside entreating of the kind witnessed by the Swan of Avon. Apart from faking insanity, the members of the Beggars Club pretended to have disabilities of all kinds: fake legs - or rather, a fake absence of leg; fake armlessness - indeed, there was one notorious member of the Club who was, to all appearances, just a head.

He would position himself in a cylindrical pit at the side of the highway, a few fellow-members would fill it in around him, and there, left visible to the innocent passer-by, was a poor fellow who by some strange means had lost his entire body yet by some semi-divine means was still able to roll to work each morning.

The Beggar's Club met in various stinking caves underneath the city – the tunnels of Chalk Farm, an abandoned well in Acton – and pool their ideas and resources. One imagines a horde of well-dressed folk going into to the meeting, chatting and joking - and a straggle of meanly-clothed and dirty scroungers emerging, legs strapped up behind them with strong leather belts, arms fastened behind their backs, their healthy limbs concealed with greasy rags.

Does the Beggar's Club exist now? It is not known. I, and probably you, have no doubt given money to a beggar under false pretences. Some signs that proclaim 'Homeless' may not be razor-sharp on their veracity. And some vendors of that fantastic But I have a personal code: honest or not, I give them all the benefit of the doubt.

The Society for the Diffusion of Useful Knowledge

Ever since the advent of the printing press it has been viewed with suspicion by the governing classes. Ink was branded 'devilish' by Bishops, and

But in 1826, leading liberal of the day Lord Brougham set about changing all that; and founded a club devoted to publishing and disseminating all kinds of 'useful knowledge' to the masses. Apparently there were great gaps in the masses' knowledge, and it was Lord Brougham's determined aim to plug them.

He had a commendable CV. Not only did he help found the Edinburgh Review in 1802, he entered parliament in 1810 and was a leading opponent of the slave trade. He was instrumental in the creation of University College, London, and rose to become Chancellor of the Exchequer. His big baby, however, was the SDUK. What sort of knowledge did the said soc. diffuse? You name it, it diffused it. Pamphlets poured from the presses of the SDUK like water from the Trevi Fountains. The masses were bombarded with so much knowledge some of them exploded. Chimneysweeps became professors overnight. Urchins were appointed surgeons after absorbing the wisdom of a mere three of Brougham's pamphlets. Humble charladies delivered profound lectures on geology after an afternoon's perusal of a couple of Brougham's 'Penny Magazines.'

I jest of course. No urchin was permitted entry to the Royal College of Surgeons to perform an appendectomy. That would have been ridiculous.

And there's the nub of the matter. The Society of the Diffusion of Useful Knowledge - inasmuch as its prime aim was to improve the mental culture of the underprivileged - was a failure, and was wound up in 1848.

Why did it fail? Because the 'lower orders' as they were then described, did not seem to want to have knowledge diffused to them, useful or otherwise. In short, they didn't buy the things. They preferred Dickens. The reason, perhaps, was the subject matter of the journals. Brougham's aim was to disseminate the latest findings of the relatively newly-established 'scientific community' to the broad hitherto-unlettered public; so the pamphlets covered such topics as Natural Theology, Nebula Theory, Uniformitarianism, etc. - in short, the new Cosmology of the Nineteenth Century which paved the way for Darwin.

It is disheartening to say the least to learn that after so many centuries of the establishment protesting against the sharing of knowledge with the broad population, that when a member of that establishment becomes enlightened and finally instigates such a thing – it is rejected.

The middle-classes were a different matter: they gobbled up the output of Charles Knight's printing presses with alacrity. But by 1848 the middle-classes were buying books, not cheap little magazines, and the SDUK folded. It had fallen into such disrepute that Thoreau, in his essay entitled 'Walking' proposed the founding of a Society for the Dissemination of Useful Ignorance.

Now there's an idea. But I think it was achieved, several decades later. I refer, of course, to the tabloid press.

MI 14 - The Pigeon Secret Service

Much has been written of the invaluable work done by our feathered cousins in the defence of these islands at time of war. Pigeons were of vital importance in the relaying of messages both in the Great War and in the '39-'45 conflict. Their names and exploits have been passed down into legend. Who has not thrilled at the courageous flight of Cher Ami, who saved the lives of 500 men who, trapped behind enemy lines, were being bombarded by both the Germans and by friendly fire? Cher Ami was despatched with the following message: *"We are along the road parallel to 276.4. Our own artillery is dropping a barrage directly on us. For heaven's sake, stop it!"* The enemy fired at the brave bird, taking both his right eye and right leg off, but the feathery fighter struggled on through the bullets and the smoke, and managed to deliver its missive. The guns were silenced, the men were rescued, and Cher Ami passed into the annals of military history. Upon return to America, Cher Ami became the mascot of the Department of Service, and was awarded the Croix de Guerre with a palm Oak

Leaf cluster. Cher Ami died at Fort Monmouth, New Jersey, on June 13, 1919 from the wounds he received in battle and was later inducted into the Racing Pigeon Hall of Fame in 1931. He was stuffed and mounted and is on permanent display in the Smithsonian Institute.

Cher Ami was, of course, American - but who has not also been humbled by reading of the winners of Britain's own Dickin Medal? Instituted in 1943 by Maria Dickin to honour the work of animals in war. the medal is a large bronze medallion, bearing the words "For Gallantry" and "We Also Serve" within a laurel wreath carried on ribbon of striped green, dark brown and pale blue. Traditionally, the medal is presented by the Lord Mayor of the City of London. It has become recognised as "the animals' Victoria Cross. As of February 2008, it has been awarded 62 times.

- 1943: Winkie - first pigeon to be awarded the medal; flew 120 miles from a crashed bomber to deliver an SOS.
- 1943: Ruhr Express - a messenger pigeon.
- 1944: Commando - a messenger pigeon.
- 1944: Paddy - messenger pigeon that made the fastest recorded crossing of the English Channel, delivering messages from Normandy for D-Day, travelling 230 miles in 4 hours 5 minutes.

- 1944: William of Orange used in Battle of Arnhem in September 1944 saving 2000 soldiers.

And yet in addition to these publicly-known achievements there is a secret, hidden group of pigeons whose work - until recently - has gone unsung, their stories untold. I refer to the Pigeon branch of the Secret Service - MI 14. Set up as a branch of the War Office, the feathered operations were codenamed *Columba*, and consisted of dozens of pigeons who - after rigorous training by the Loftsmen of the Royal Signals corp. - were dropped in the heart of enemy Germany carrying miniature spying kits. The above listed Winkie was a notable member of this elite club of avian adventurers, as was William of Orange and GI Joe. This was not, however, an exclusively male corp.: the exploits of plucky Devonian dove Mary of Exeter found their way too into the classified archives of the Intelligence Service. Perhaps the most heroic star of MI 14, however, was William of Orange, who in 1944 saved 2000 lives at the Battle of Arnhem. The airborne operation were surrounded by Germans, and with their radio sets out of action, their only hope of communicating with HQ was by air. William was released at 10.30 am on September 9th 1944, and arrived home with his message at 2.55 - travelling an astonishing 250 miles. As a result of his valiant achievement he was awarded the Dickin medal, and according to his owner Sir William Proctor Smith of Cheshire, became Grandfather to many racing pigeons.

According to the authorities, the feathered section of the Intelligence Service was wound up in 1946. But if you happen to glance skyward one summer's day, and chance to spot a pigeon carrying a small pair of binoculars, a tiny codebook, and a digital camera - pause awhile, and wish him God speed. Don't ask him where he's off to, though. If he told you, he'd probably have to peck you to death afterwards.

The great Winkie, in dress uniform.

The Bilderberg Group

To have written a book on strange clubs and not included in the miscellany of eccentricity an association that some have described – and you know who you are – as perhaps the most notorious and secretive society of all, would smack, quite frankly, of insanity.

 'Notorious yet secretive? Something of an oxymoron!' I hear you say. I didn't actually hear you. I'm not telepathic. 'You are correct!' I reply. For over the years, like the Freemasons, this club has become famous throughout the world - for being secret. And like the masons it has attracted the wildest of speculations as to its nature, function and purpose: all of which hyperbolic attributions can never – because of it very secrecy – be challenged or refuted. Such has been the range of its members – veering wildly from General Eisenhower to left-wing British politician Denis Healey - that surely no one political shading can be applied to the Society. Ostensibly it has acted as a Steering Committee for the Western world. And judging from the way the

Western World has veered and tottered blindly into the twenty-first century like a myopic mule, it would appear that the Bilderberg Group's captaincy of our fate has been singularly lacking in what might describe as 'navigational nonce.'

It was founded at the outset of the Cold War. Upon origination, its first conference was held at the Hotel de Bilderberg near Arnhem in the Netherlands from 29th May to 31st May 1954, having been initiated by the Polish politician Josef Retinger who was concerned with the growth of Anti-Americanism in Western Europe. To redress this, and to promote the cause of Atlanticism, the Group voted to meet thereafter on an annual basis, and for those encounters not to be open to the public. Thus the mystique of the club was born.

Its purpose? Well, quite clearly the Bilderberg Group has acted as a kind of steering committee of the West, a pooling of ideas of the great and good. And perhaps bad. Its membership has ranged vastly from obscure European royalty to left-wing British politicians , Teutonic Social Democrats, and representatives of international business. Such a broad church might indicate to the conspiracists that Bilderberg is far from being one single political shade. They meet behind closed doors and the press is not permitted.

So who knows what Bilderberg actually does? Perhaps they all pretend to discuss things of international import, relishing the notoriety their club has garnered whilst all the time - the doors having been locked and the security guards installed – sitting round a big table and discussing fancy mice, cigarette cards, or egg-cups.

In my investigations I managed to secure an interview with a member of this august and mysterious enclave and am willing now to publish my findings. Admittedly, my subject did not rank incredibly highly in the hierarchy of Bilderberg. In fact, he is in charge of the catering. I will call him 'Edwin Stanforth,' – for that, indeed, is his name; and his revelations about the inner workings of Bilderberg are being printed here for the first time.

According to Mr. Stanforth, the founding member of Bilderberg Prince Berhard of the Netherlands was extremely fond of lemon and ginger tea, whilst Head of Nato Alexander Haig was a martyr to cup cakes. Denis Healey was a confirmed Bovril man, whilst Bill Gates was never able to suppress his enthusiasm for an espresso macchiato accompanied by a small plateful of custard creams.

Bill Clinton waived his right to a full spread, choosing instead to plump for a humble madelaine cake with a jug of sparkling water; whilst Queen Sofia of Spain insisted – somewhat unorthodoxly – on a full English breakfast prior to each discussion on economic matters. Enoch Powell: Ovaltine. German Chancellor Helmut Schmidt – Greek Salad and a side-order of chorizo sausage: while Beyarni Benediktsson, Mayor of Reyjkayvik, could not commence even the most trivial of committee meetings without first being refreshed by a steaming mug of Earl Grey and a hob-nob.

I am conscious that some of you may not be overly impressed with these findings. Be lenient. I have only just commenced on this career as an investigative journalist, and am fully aware that what the Portuguese Minister for the Economy had during his tea-break may not deserve to attract the same enthusiasm as, say, the Watergate revelations. I'm sorry. But the fact is they wouldn't let me in. I met Mr. Stanforth in a nearby Hotel and, after a few pina coladas and a cheeky Chablis, was able to extract the above tit-bits.

But watch this space. There may be more. I've just spotted the Vice-chairman of the Slovak Chamber of Commerce in the snug bar, and if I can get at him over a quiet Guinness, who knows what he might divulge. *'Olaf! Olaf!'*

Printed in Great Britain
by Amazon